By Julian Goodson

Photo Credit: June Behrendt, Reflections Photography

It is easier to build strong children than to repair broken men.

- Fredrick Douglass

In loving memory of Uncle Leroy.

Love and constructive criticism don't always get along very well.

- Julian Goodson

For my wife, Stacey, who never let me settle for anything less than the level of my own expectations.

Table of Contents

FOREWARD

"Aging out." He kept referring to these foster kids who turn 18 and "age out of the system." It was a problem I had never considered. Honestly, foster care in general was something I had never really considered.

I was an executive at a Christian non-profit who built homes for families and he was a social worker who worked with young people. "These young people need job training, help getting their diploma or GED and even help finding housing." Housing? Yup.

Many of these young people reach adulthood and the benefits from the state, to foster-parents, cease. No more checks. No more reimbursements. That means an 18 year old (who has already faced a lifetime of challenges) ends up on the street or sleeping on friend's front porches. Couch surfing.

The conversation shook me. Short-term, it led to establishing a program to help deliver job training through helping us build homes, and even a diploma or GED but the housing issue wasn't part of the deal. What does society do with these kids who still need so much? They are, on paper, adults. But I remember myself at 18, so young and naive--and I had a healthy upbringing, with my Mom, Dad and many siblings under our roof!

At that same time my wife began working at the local children's hospital and many of her patients were being treated due to "non-accidental trauma." Often, they were wards of the state. These stories were heartbreaking and she talked about how much she wanted to bring these little ones home to love them. My experience with the back end of foster care was now bumping into her experience with the front.

These stories were hard to shake. Then, when our attempts for having another child ended with tears, we knew what had to happen. As a Christian I know God isn't in the accident business: He has a plan. Even our suffering and pain could be used for our good and for His glory. We had an extra bedroom and plenty of love to go around. It was time to open our home to a child in the foster care system.

Fast forward a few years and we've had the pleasure of one, short placement and some "sub-care" here and there (basically babysitting for other foster parents who are travelling). It's not all that much. We're open to adopting if it comes to that. It's been mostly great with plenty of both laughter and tears. But from the entire journey the best part for me was meeting Julian and Stacey Goodson.

Stacey taught one of the required classes for foster parents. When my wife recognized the Goodsons lived around the corner from us we decided we needed to get to know them over dinner. Turns out Julian was working for the fella who first told me about kids "aging out." Small world. All four of us were passionate about our city and its young people and we were instant friends.

Since then I've seen the best example of what foster care and adoption looks like in the Goodsons. They have a full house of kids from various backgrounds. It's beautiful!

As a pastor, there is very little in my life more satisfying than seeing people who make God's agenda their own agenda. Replacing their own desires with His desires, often at great cost. That is sacrificial love: love that costs you something to give it. It's what the Goodsons do every day--not only at home but with where they choose to live and even with their careers.

Seriously, they picked our city because they are a mixed race home and they wanted a place that had diversity. Did you catch that? They didn't drive out to the suburbs even though the larger floor plan and blue ribbon schools can be very attractive. They chose to plant their family in a neighborhood, near the High School so they could be fully invested in the community. They chose to go where they could make the most difference.

They both could be making more money in other fields but they both choose to work around young people who need caring adult relationships. They both serve as volunteer coaches and advocates for foster care and adoption. In short, they walk the walk.

So why do they do it? Well, that's why Julian wrote this book. You'll get to read his story and you'll see how you can make a difference and be a part of the solution too. Whether you are considering a career in social work, providing foster care or even donating backpacks to students in the fall, there is *something* you can do to help. *Thoughts of a Foster Dad* will help provide you with some "next steps."

Be prepared because Julian's story will inspire, challenge and educate you. I'm honored to call him my friend and I know you will benefit from all the pages that follow.

Christopher Hall

Introduction

Imagine there is a little boy named Johnny in your neighborhood. Johnny appears to be about twelve years old when you see him bouncing around. You notice him everywhere; at the grocery store, the ice cream shop and at the school where your kids attend. You find it interesting that every time you see Johnny he is wearing worn-out blue jeans, tattered sneakers, and a dingy Detroit Lions hoodie. One day he walks up to your front door with a rake in hand and asks to clean your yard for some cash. You oblige, of course, and after he finishes, you hand him a crisp ten-dollar bill. The next time you see Johnny, he is at the corner store hanging with three other neighborhood kids yelling at a kid while grabbing another kid by his shirt collar. His arm is cocked back and his fist is balled up: he is going to slug the other kid. You realize its Johnny because you noticed the same dingy Lions hoodie.

A couple of weeks later, you arrive to pick your kids up from the high school football game and you notice Johnny hanging out. Again, you recognize him from the now tattered and dingy Lions hoodie. The game is over. He appears to be loitering around the school without anything to do. You think nothing of it - surely his mom is coming to get him. Surely this is a one-time thing; Johnny would never hang out with "those kids."

Your mind drifts to thoughts of unruly neighborhood kids, the "thugs" you wish would just go away. You try not to think of Johnny as one of them, but it is becoming impossible to not imagine that dingy Detroit hoodie among them. Later that night, you run out to the corner store and notice police lights where Johnny lives. You think to yourself, "It is probably just a domestic dispute or something, I'm going to keep it moving."

A couple of weeks pass by and life goes on. A month passes, and you begin to notice that the leaves are starting to blanket the grass in your yard again. You bitterly think to yourself, "Where is Johnny when I need him?"

The season changes from fall to winter; spring back to summer; summer back to fall and the next time Johnny crosses your mind is when you plop down on your couch to watch the Lions' season opener on a brisk, Sunday afternoon.

What happened to Johnny?

Child Protective Services was contacted over and over again; too many times they went to Johnny's school as well as the home that he shared with his mother and two-year-old half-brother. One day, CPS finally removed Johnny and his brother from their mother and took them to a temporary shelter home where he anxiously awaited the "social worker lady" to come back. He only wanted to know when he could go back to live with his mom, even though he knew that living with her wasn't safe.

At the temporary shelter, Johnny waited and waited. Days turned into weeks and weeks turned into months before he heard anything. Eventually, he was moved into a residential facility where CPS places children when foster homes can't be found for them; he was thankful that his little brother was able to go to a foster home. The foster parents seemed like really nice people and he felt so lucky when they brought his brother to visit. His brother got to visit his biological father and extended family. Meanwhile, Johnny never got a call or visit from them.

His visits with his brother's foster family and the knowledge of the connection his brother has with his foster family makes him wonder:

Why don't they want me too?

Am I not good enough?

Am I too old?

Johnny has been living in the residential facility for a year now and just turned fifteen. He struggles significantly with anger management, does not trust the people in his life, and constantly struggles in building relationships. Many potential families have inquired about him, but become "scared off" by his behaviors at the residential facility and his lack of progress at school. Every time a family walks away, he is left in a state of depression, again and again. His feelings of desperation and rejection continue to swallow him, leaving him completely isolated and lonely.

He continues to wonder to himself, "Why doesn't anybody want me? Am I not loveable enough?"

If you have ever had the pleasure of meeting Johnny, you might ask him what he likes to do. He will tell you he likes to watch Detroit Lions football. Not because he likes football, because the tattered, dingy, Lions hoodie is the last birthday gift that his mom gave him before she was removed from his life.

Johnny wants and needs a strong, compassionate, and patient family to love him. Every kid coming out of foster care does. In the years since I started my journey, I've learned every single child has a story to share and simply wants someone who will listen; someone who will love them after they have articulated everything within them. I wrote this book to illustrate the human side of the foster care system – an entity that is too often explained through statistics, systems, and laws. And despite the extreme importance of these outcomes, it often sweeps the very individuality of the persons within this system under the rug.

We all need to know the stories behind these invisible children. Someone needs to know the harm our biases and stereotypes of youth in the foster care system is having on our young people.

This book is a series of stories about my life, intertwined with experiences from my work in foster care and adoption, combined with the many life-experiences of children who enter into foster care. At the conclusion of each chapter, you will find a section that explains the connections in my life to foster care that lead to my "key beliefs" as well as "takeaways" from my experience as a foster dad.

There are poems used throughout this book. These poems were written with a spoken word theme to them. Prior to reading them, if you are not familiar with spoken word or "poetry slams," please take a moment to search for clips on YouTube. In addition to the poems themselves, I also discuss why I feel spoken word and poetry are amazing art forms. It has been a very therapeutic form of expression for me to better understand my thoughts and emotions.

I hope you enjoy reading and pondering, "Thoughts of a Foster Dad."

Chapter 1 - Ernie's Barbershop

Did you know?

There are approximately 415,000 children in the Foster Care System in the United States.

November 22, 2014

"Julian, Jason wants to know if it's okay that he calls you dad," asked our foster son, Carter. Jason quickly followed by asking, "Stacey, Carter wants to know if it's okay that he calls you mom."

My wife Stacey and I look sideways at each other, knowing that Carter would never call Stacey mom. We know there is a battle within him; deciding whether he will allow himself to ever love us. Carter is still very close to his birth mom and holds a deep love for her, in spite of the abuse and neglect, his only goal is reunification with her.

However, Jason is a lot different. Coming from a lockdown residential facility, he has only been in our home for three weeks.

Already, he is showing signs of longing for the traditional parental bonds that he longs for and misses. He craves it. He wants it. He needs it. However, he would never come out and tell us that.

Still confused by the original questions from Jason and Carter, I pile our six kids into the vehicle for a visit to Ernie's Barbershop. As we drive through the neighborhood, I can see Jason taking it all in.

Ernie's Barbershop is located in Southeast Grand Rapids, across the street from Sam's Market, which is really just a glorified liquor store. Next door is a makeshift dollar store specializing in black hair products and the entire building is in need of a serious face-lift; it has this permanent grimy feel to it.

Ernie's Barbershop is the longest standing business on the block and it is still Black owned. It stands as this beacon of Black entrepreneurship and longevity amongst churches, liquor stores, and gas stations that are all owned and operated by White or Middle Eastern families. My dad took me to Ernie's to get my first haircut as a shorty, so it's fitting that I take my sons to do the same.

To get inside of Ernie's you have to walk next to what looks like an auto-body shop. There always seems to be activity inside but I have never actually seen a car being fixed. Ernie's itself is in need of some updates and a coat of fresh paint and I'm convinced that the same mustard-brown colored floors have been there for at least thirty years. The shop has a giant old-school glass picture window, but despite the dusty rays of light streaming through it, the lighting inside the shop is always dim. Posters of local promoters pushing their latest club parties are splattered on the walls, covering up most of the chipped paint. But you don't go to barbershops for the aesthetics, you go for the conversation. Ernie's Barbershop may need a little T.L.C., but the chatter in the shop doesn't need any assistance – it is electric!

The barbershop is a very unique place where a father and a son can bond. The stories that are told by other patrons are epic - a lot of "exaggerated truths," if you will.

That day at Ernie's Barbershop, after being greeted by high-fives, daps (or fist pounds), and bro-man hugs, I introduced Jason to my barber and everyone else in the shop as my son. It was the first time I had ever introduced him to anyone that way and, though he didn't see me paying attention, I saw him become visibly giddy and I could hardly contain a quick smile. He sat there in the barber chair and relished being a part of something; our family, this place, our community. His chubby cheeks, fat dimples, and braided cornrows jiggled as they plunged deeper into the chair to get a line-up. His expressions let me know that he was thrilled to be there. At that moment, my thoughts were clear, my actions pure, and my feelings were prideful.

Right on cue, Carter asked the perfect barbershop question. "Julian, if you could pay to see any QB in the NFL right now, who would it be?" Looking up at the fifty-inch flat screen on the grimy beige wall, I see highlights from Russell Wilson and without hesitation, I blurt out "Russell Wilson." The shop erupts as grown men, including the barbers, yell out their picks.

Brady.

Kaepernick.

Breeze.

Manning.

Some Lions homer even said Stafford.

Carter sat in Trey's chair getting his mini-afro shaped up perfectly. He was totally feeling a bit smug, as he just asked the perfect question, getting a knee-jerk response from everyone. His attention-seeking actions were validated positively.

Eric, one of the barbers, walks in carrying a plastic bag with a styrofoam box from Auntie Dees. The smell of smothered chicken, mac-n-cheese, and collard greens permeated the air and the scent of soul food made my stomach jump. Instantly, the whole barbershop seemed to become hungry. There was never a dull moment at Ernie's.

I believe that every young male needs to be introduced to a well-known and respected barber. There is something very therapeutic about going to see your favorite barber. My barber's name is Will. We have known each other since the seventh grade and graduated from Ottawa Hills High School together. Even though I rock a bald head, I still enjoy sitting in his chair to get cleaned up. Will knows me very well, so he knows that Jason is a foster son and not my biological child.

"What's your name, son?" Will asks as Jason settles into his chair.

"Jason, but my friends call me JJ," he replies with a smile on his face.

Will turns to me in passive curiosity, "Ole Mo," he calls me by my childhood nickname, "he just visiting?"

I try to answer as nonchalantly as possible, "Nah he'll be with me for a lil bit."

Will's eyebrows perk up. "Oh, he a part of 'the Program'?"

I nod in agreement. "Yeah," trying to think of an equally profound and fitting name for the children who have entered our home. "#TeamGoodson" I shout with a smile.

#TheProgram and #TeamGoodson describe the roles I play as father to all of these children and even some of their friends - two of which have fathers that are completely out of the picture. In all, there are nine teenage boys that are a part of #TheProgram: my biological son Gunnor and his friend Jamie, my foster son Carter, my two adopted sons Andre and Michael, Andre's two friends Steph and Derek, Darrin, and now Jason. I often joke that I have enough sons to start my own basketball team. But, on the day we visited the barbershop, there were six of them - Gunnor, Carter, Michael, Andre, Derek and Jason were all joining me on this adventure.

During our conversation, the barbershop had fallen silent as everyone was listening in, or "ear hustling." The barbers in the shop all knew I was a foster dad, but I could sense the confusion of the other patrons whose ears had perked up to follow this interesting exchange.

"Wow, how many kids does this dude have?" said the faces of the men waiting their turn. In a weird way, their confusion validated my pride and only encouraged me to talk more about our family, this "Program," as they had called it.

Now, you have to understand the situation in order to understand this pride. I am a black man surrounded by other black men in a barbershop located in the "hood;" a location where it is common place to not be in your child's life. In a setting such as this, conversations about child support, baby momma drama, and non-custodial parenting are the norm. On that day, in that barbershop, I considered it safe to say that I was the only man there who would willingly sign-up to take care of *someone else's* kid.

So at the risk of sounding, self-righteous or condescending, I continued. I loved being able to show versatility in my communication skills. While speaking a colorful language laced with plenty of slang, I was able to remain a role model for my teenage boys and maintain my professionalism, letting everyone in the shop know, "yeah, I still have my ghetto-pass."

"Man, Ole Mo, it takes a real man to step up and take care of someone else's kid. I admire you for it," Trey, the barber fixing Carter up, says adamantly.

As he says this, my eyes fixated on Jason and his smile disappears. My mind spins.

Was he nervous?

Was he excited?

Was he angry?

Was he made to feel like a charity case in that instance?

I knew I had to think of a quick comeback to acknowledge Trey's response.

Remaining calm, I energetically respond, "Yo, Trey, that 'IS' my kid, bro. He look just like me; can't you see the resemblance?" As everyone in the shop begins to laugh, Jason's smile starts to return.

Two things came out of that exchange: 1) Trey had no idea the type of damage a comment like that can have on a fifteen-year-old kid and, 2) I had to be sure that I validated both Jason and Trey's thoughts, comments and feelings. Trey is a good dude, a long-time buddy that I respect and admire. He had no ill-intent because he was just giving me props and, in the end, I truly appreciated the gesture. But situations like this can be defining moments in a foster parent's relationship with their child. My comment was meant to diffuse what could have been a very embarrassing situation for Jason and make him feel safe again. I hope my joke made him feel loved and included. Foster kids struggle with a sense of belonging, they struggle with fitting in with a family they don't really know. For Jason, all of these feelings were compounded by the fact that he was a fifteen-year-old boy. I can't stress enough the importance of loving and including all of the children that you parent as your own and show them how much they do belong and are wanted.

I pride myself not only on being a good foster dad but a good parent as well, and I go out of my way to share my stories about my experiences – even with a complete stranger. People need to know that you can have a loving family with kids that you didn't father. To me, being a foster dad is natural.

When I hear comments such as Trey's, I experience a wave of different emotions, reactions, and thoughts. If that comment would've been made without my sons being present, it would have gone a lot differently. I might have responded with something like, "I'm just doing God's work by answering a calling," or tell them that the kids are just a part of #TheProgram and that they all have to eat. People often respond by saying, "I commend you Julian, you're doing good work." "You are crazy for having all those teenage boys in your house." "There is no way I'd do that." I heard a lot of these comments during our visit to Ernie's, but I left the barbershop wondering what the people in the shop that day really thought of me.

Thoughts of a Foster Dad: Key Beliefs and Takeaways

- All kids, especially teenage boys need an experience like the barbershop with their father or a male-role-model. There is an indescribable bonding experience when a father takes his son to get a fresh cut. After the cut, he looks at himself in the mirror and a transformation takes place - he feels good about himself. A father can validate him by simply telling him "you look good son," or "you look like a million bucks." This holds especially true for a foster kid. It was an expensive trip to the barbershop that day, but the bonding and the connection that came out of it was priceless.

- No kid wants to be labeled as a foster kid. So, don't label them. That label can make them feel like a charity case and can ruin their self-esteem.

- All kids need to be told that they are beautiful on a consistent basis, with words and actions. Whether it is a trip to the barbershop or the beauty salon, they need to feel and be told that they look good. These moments can be become very special events that can be capitalized upon and improve not only your relationship with the child but their self-esteem as well.

- Spending time and mentoring your kids' friends is more time to build them up in a safe environment. This act demonstrates foster kids know that you care about them and their world enough to be involved. You are engaged with their day-to-day activities. Instead of simply dropping a friend off at his house, stop and get ice cream first. Making friends feel welcomed will go a long way in making your foster kid feel welcome too.

Chapter 2: 1010 Eastern

It's in the numbers!

"Over 40% of males formerly in foster care reported contact with the Criminal Justice System."

The Beginning: Why I do what I do

Spring 1984

It was a Tuesday afternoon and I had just plopped down on the shag green carpet in our living room, exhausted after a long day at school. I was sporting a black Adidas polyester jumpsuit with the matching red and white shell-toe Adidas tennis shoes. My Sony Walkman was banging "It's Tricky" by Run DMC. It was definitely the eighties and I was definitely "living it up."

Procrastinating doing my real homework, I turned on Scooby Doo and began flipping through the Grand Rapids Press aimlessly searching for an article to show my dad when he got home. "Son, it is important to stay up on current events," he would always say before asking me to write a reflection on newspaper articles.

Despite the annoyance of this project, these little essays were all about making me a better reader and, eventually, writer.

My lazy afternoon was disrupted, however, when out of the corner of my eye, I saw a scruffy little mouse dart out from the register in the living room and jet behind the garbage in the kitchen. I jumped out of my spot in disgust.

"I hate mice!" I mumbled to myself, equally as disgusted with the fact that my fear of mice had rendered me frozen in my spot. Alert, I take in more of my surroundings. On the dining room table is a worn, dingy, yellow plastic container overflowing with tobacco – a scent so strong it permeates the room. I try to refocus on my newspaper.

"And I would've gotten away with it if weren't for those nosy kids," sounds the television in the background.

Just as I was settling in, there was a knock on the door. As I got closer, I saw that it was my 5th-grade teacher from Alexander Elementary, Mr. Smith. He was a popular teacher in the school amongst the students and staff, but when seeing him on my porch, all I could think was, "Am I in trouble? What is he doing here?"

"Julian?" Mr. Smith says, looking surprised to see me. "What are you doing here?"

"I live here. What are you doing here?" I stuttered.

"I'm here to...umm. Well, is Big Mack here?" stammered my teacher. His eyes shifted away from me as he slumped against the doorframe.

"Yeah," I responded. "Am I in trouble?"

He smiled visibly relaxing and said, "no."

"Dad! Mr. Smith is here!" I called out, feeling a little better.

I stepped back to let Mr. Smith through the door and saw my best friend, Buster, standing behind him with his basketball in hand. Checking to make sure my dad was on the way, I went outside with Buster to shoot some hoops.

"What is Mr. Smith doing here?" Buster asks.

I shrugged. "I don't know," I truthfully responded.

After a couple of basketball games of Fight 21, we decided to go to Fannie's Corner to get some snacks. I quickly ran inside, saw that Mr. Smith was gone, but that there was now money on the table next to the bowl of tobacco.

I meekly muttered, "Dad...can I have some money? Me and Bus wanna go to Fannie's and grab some snacks and play some video games."

Without looking at me, he handed me a ten dollar bill off the table and barked, "Be back by dark."

Later on, Buster and I continued to wonder about Mr. Smith's visit.

"What do you think Mr. Smith wanted?" Buster asked again over a video game controller.

As I handled the controller smashing the fire button repeatedly with one life left in Dig-Dug, I replied, "I have no idea. I hope I'm not in trouble."

The next day at school, I nervously looked to Mr. Smith hoping to see what was really in store for me. All of my fears came true when, after the class roll call, Mr. Smith said, "Mr. Goodson come to my desk." I visibly cringed and began slowly walking up to him. When I got to his desk, I was surprised when his face lit up with a grin and he said, "I need you to be my helper for the day." As surprised as I was, I was even more delighted, casually brushing off the awkwardness of the situation.

After another long day, I got home and settled into my spot on the floor. My mom handed me my afternoon snack - fried ring bologna dipped in ketchup. She settled into her spot on the couch, my dad was in his chair chillin'. It was Wednesday and I hated Wednesdays because that was the day my mom went to Dialysis Center of West Michigan due to her diabetes, which explained why there was always hard rock candy around. Her favorites were Jolly Ranchers and peppermints. When she went for dialysis, it constantly seemed like she was in a bad mood – she would always make me do everything.

"Julian, wash the dishes."

"Julian, vacuum the floor."

"Julian, rub my back."

A knock on the door interrupted my thoughts. I went to the door and a man I didn't know asked for Big Mack.

"Dad, someone is here for you!" I yelled.

"Ok. Send him in." My dad barked back.

As the man passed into the doorway, I noticed a big navy blue truck without windows across the street. Odd, but my street, Eastern, was weird to me because across the street from our house is where the graveyard started. It was also a busy street so I returned to my seat, not thinking too much about it.

As the man left, I got up to shut the heavy wood door with a steel deadbolt. Before I sat down, I swiftly grabbed my plate and walked towards the sink to put it away, cautiously hoping that I wouldn't see a mouse in the kitchen again. As I was walking, I looked out the window in the kitchen and notice a man carrying a black club with a shield on his face and then noticed more men walking quickly in front of him. All of a sudden…. "KAAAAAAAABOOM!!!"

I heard a loud, earth-shattering crash sounding like there was a thunderstorm in the front room.

"PUT YOUR MUTHAPHUCKIN HANDS WHERE I CAN SEE THEM!!!" someone screamed.

I dropped the plate that I had been carrying, and it loudly shattered onto the floor as a white man wearing a blue "SWAT" uniform put a gun right in my face. Scared shitless, I put my hands where he could see them. Standing still, I could hear screams coming from the front room.

"Where is Mack Goodson? We have a search warrant," the man in the blue uniform yelled at me. After realizing that I was only a child and not a threat, he took me into the living room with my parents and my sister, Cindy. I sat on my mom's lap and she whispered to me, "take a deep breath, stay alert, and by all means do whatever the officer says." I meekly looked up at my dad and he stared back at me.

He finally said, "Don't worry they are only here for me and everything will be okay." You would think that in that moment that he would have been rattled but he had the same cool, calm, and collected demeanor that I had come to know. The SWAT team handcuffed him, put him in the back of the police car, and drove off. My adrenaline was running so high that I thought my heart would beat out of my chest. However, I felt assured, because I believed my dad when he told me everything would be okay.

What I hadn't known before the raid was that the worn, dingy, yellow plastic container on the table wasn't full of tobacco but rather something called weed. The man that had left prior had bought the whole 2 pounds and my mom had taken the $2,000 cash to the safe downstairs in the basement, the police didn't get that. That day, I learned that the funny smelling smoke coming from those rolled up cigarettes was illegal; up until then I had been clueless because it was so common in my house. I was a kid, I thought everyone smoked Zig Zag cigarettes and it was totally normal.

The next morning, my dad made bail and came home. He told me again that everything would be okay and I believed him. We never talked about it again.

Our house was raided three more times in the next two years.

Two years later, as a young fourteen-year-old boy, I lost my mom to diabetes. I used to believe that if I loved her with all of my might, if I loved her with everything that I had, if I loved her more than the next breath that I'd take, then she would live forever. I was devastated by her death.

The youngest of four children, I had plenty of support and of course, my family was there for me. My brother Derek, and sister Tracey were both in their mid-twenties and my sister, Cindy had just turned eighteen. In spite of the wisdom and support of my siblings and other family members, no one was there for me like my two cousins, Ryan and Marcus. For two weeks they didn't leave my side.

My roll-dogs, my two best friends, Buster and Lyonel aka Swell, picked me up at school as I walked around Ottawa Hills High School like a zombie. Swell and Tyreece came to scoop me up and take me to Paul I Phillips Gym to hoop. My neighborhood crew of friends Vonte, Troy, Greg and Chris, Karl and Parnell (Spud) all came to get me and tried to keep me busy. It was like this for about a month. I always had someone in my corner making sure that I was good and preoccupied, but then that support system that was once so strong, slowly but surely started to dissipate.

All of my siblings had children and lives to continue living and they went back to their everyday problems. My friends were still in my corner; however, it seemed that everyone fell back into their normal routines. I began to realize after about three months had passed, that I hadn't seen my dad. He worked road construction on the east side of the state so it was normal for me to go long stretches without seeing him. I had never felt so alone in all my life. My house went from buzzing and loving with all types of people around, to dark and dreary – being overrun by mice and vermin. Summertime came and I walked to the overstuffed mailbox to get the mail. It hadn't been checked in weeks. As I opened the box, I noticed a shutoff notice for the lights and the water as well as a letter from my dad addressed to me and my sister, Cindy. Thankfully, his letter contained a check to pay some bills.

That summer there were many firsts: it was my first experience ever going to a utility place to pay a shutoff notice and it was the first time going to the grocery store to buy food for myself. That summer was the first time that I had ever cooked dinner for myself and eaten alone. To this very day, I have a hard time eating alone. For months, I lived at that mice and roach infested house because it was my childhood home and I had never lived anywhere else. For months I lived alone at 1010 Eastern, unsupervised. One day a pipe burst in the ceiling and I couldn't get it to stop. Cindy was in tears and she was on the phone screaming to someone that it was raining in the living room. The next day the phone was cut off and I found myself going next door just to use the phone. Without the house, my stability would be completely gone.

Before my mom died she made me promise that I'd go to school and attend college. College was the furthest thing from my mind but I went to school every day, mainly so that I would have something to eat and wouldn't be alone. But one of the biggest reasons I went every day was so I could play sports. I turned to sports and found them to be my true escape. The summer brought out some pretty intense baseball leagues for the inner-city kids. Teddy Raspberry field on Jefferson Street was electric with the Mid-City baseball youth leagues.

But it was the 80's and crack-cocaine was turning my neighborhood upside down. It seemed that overnight, my school-friends turned into glorified drug dealers with a chip on their shoulders and something to prove. My dad's reputation preceded me so "wanna-be-thugs" and overnight-studio-gangsters came from all directions trying to recruit me to be on their drug team. Apparently, they all knew that my dad was the biggest dealer on this side of the state and they thought that I was of the age to "carry on" the family business. The streets were watching and talking. Nickel and dime street peddlers wanted his "plug and connect" (his plug being his dealer and his connect being his distributors and workers). What these dealers didn't know, was that I was much bigger than that life and I had ZERO desire to go that route. Seeing my house get raided scared me straight.

My walk to the bus stop to get to school was no picnic. I would witness drug-transactions constantly. Cadillac's with tinted windows and Nissan trucks with chromed-out hammer wheels flooded the streets. Suzuki 4x4, Tonka Toy looking trucks, banging stereo systems, beating the latest from Chubb Rock and Heavy D heavily influenced the neighborhood boys. Neighbors left but the hood remained. One day, Vonte rolled up in the Diamante with the vogues on them and asked me if I wanted a ride to school, it looked like he hadn't slept yet. Baseheads greeted me on the way to school! This was all too normal and I was just trying to survive.

On the outside, I had it all together. But organized chaos and confusion lived inside of me. It consumed me every day. I was a shell of myself at school. My grades slipped but my love for basketball forced me to make that 2.0-grade point average in order to stay on the team. There were days when I would go to school and the basketball court was the safest place I had. The late bus ride home was horrible because I knew I was going home to an empty house with mice running through it. In two short years, I went from this happy-go-lucky kid hoopin' in the back yard with my friends to having to deal with real-life scenarios that would bring most adults to their knees. Temptation was all around me, and then one day, it all changed.

Aunt Carol to the rescue!

One day Aunt Carol came to pick me up to take me school shopping and then to drop me off at my part-time job at McDonalds. Sitting in my driveway before leaving she simply asked me, "Julian, how are you kiddo?" Tears flowed! All I could do was cry. When she asked me what was wrong I cried harder.

"Theerrethererr thereree was aaa moumommouuse in in in the ceccceereaall." I wailed.

"What? There was a what?" She asked with an anxious tone; almost as if she knew she wouldn't believe the answer.

After composing myself, but still breathing hard I said, "There was a mouse in my cereal."

I lost it and could no longer deal with it all. I hadn't seen my dad in months and when I did, he just gave me some money and told me to get what I needed. This was helpful, but what I really needed was a hug. What I really needed was some nurturing. What I really needed was some love. What I really needed and wanted was my mom. And there I was, sitting next to a woman that looked, smelled, and talked just like her. In that moment, I needed my aunt and she knew it.

With tears streaming down my face I asked, "Can I go to your house?" The cloud was much too dark. The demons were much too loud. I told her "Auntie, I cannot go back in that house."

She muttered under her breath, "I knew I should've called CPS. Somebody is going to OD."

"What is CPS?" I whispered.

She said, "Julian go in the house and get whatever you need to get."

"Auntie, No! I'm not going back in there." I screamed.

That day I left 1010 Eastern with nothing but the clothes on my back and completely abandoned the property. Unfortunately, it wouldn't be the last time I walked out of my house with just the clothes on my back.

Later, my Aunt Carol took me shopping at Steketee's Department Store on 28th street and then got me something to eat. I told her that I needed some structure, someone to challenge me and hold me accountable for my goals and responsibilities. I craved the relationship I had with my parents growing up and I knew that my Uncle Leroy and she could provide it.

"Auntie" as I called her, had a discussion with my Uncle and they decided to let me come and live there until....well...until the next thing happened. Whatever that might've been; there wasn't a timetable. That day my cousins Marcus and Ryan became my brothers and their little sister Melanie became my sister. I went to sleep that night a little on edge, waking up in the middle of the night to use the bathroom and get a drink of water. For the first time in two years, I went into a kitchen in the middle of the night and a mouse didn't jump from behind something and scare the shit out of me. I smiled as I went back to bed, finally able to relax. I slept like a rock and woke up the next morning to the smell of bacon – the best alarm clock ever. At that moment, I knew my life had changed. I walked into Ottawa Hills High School with a fresh new haircut, a new shirt, new pants, new socks, even my Fruit of the Looms were new. I felt like a new person. I stepped off the bus and went into the school with a new mission. It was the start of my senior year.

My GPA the year prior was a dismal 1.5. My senior year I finished with a 3.5. Hmm...I wonder why.

My Aunt and Uncle, Carol and Leroy have been married now for over fifty years. They are well respected in the educational field in Grand Rapids, Michigan. Aunt Carol taught for Grand Rapids Public Schools for over fifteen years before moving on to become a principal for another twenty years. Uncle Leroy retired from Grand Rapids Community College as a school counselor after over thirty years of service. They were educators and I couldn't have landed in a better place. They also adopted both Marcus and Ryan as toddlers so they were already doing God's work. I imagine taking in their nephew was an easy decision.

The day Aunt Carol came to pick me up to take me school shopping and witnessed my meltdown was the day I was introduced to foster care. Was I removed? No. Was Child Protective Services ever called? No. Was I neglected? Yes. Was I traumatized? Yes. I often wonder what would've happened to me had they not taken me in. It's a scary thought. That summer, five of my childhood friends were murdered, dozens more went to prison, and some are still serving time. I was in the middle of all of it. I was swirling around in the middle of a life-storm that burned blocks, pummeled parks, and destroyed almost everything in its path. If it had not been for them I could've been swept away by the storm. Luckily, I had a strong family that picked me up.

But what about the child that goes through similar situations without that support system? There are hundreds of thousands of stories like mine that don't end with a great aunt and uncle. In essence, my aunt and uncle became my foster parents. They stepped into my life at a time of crisis. They are a big part of the reason why I didn't fall into the "hood-traps." They are a big part of the reason why I finished high school and went to college. Because of them, I truly believe that foster parents are some of the most important people on the planet.

Spoken words of a Foster Dad

This is one of the first spoken word poems that I wrote and posted to social media.

"I'm an emotional train wreck right now and for those of you that know me...pray for me! This is for everyone that has a mother to love!

Mother's Day

Guidance, support, security, safety, love!
A mother is the most important person on the planet.
Sorry Obama, but Michelle got you beat,
Because the tender touches of a mother is so sweet.
When scrapes, bumps and bruises come into play,
A mother knows how to kiss the pain away.

When you fall off that bike and skin that knee,
Mom will not only pray on it,
But she gets out the peroxide and puts a Band-Aid on it.
Now I'm a 14-year-old teenager and the cards
Gave us a hand that's short, she was my joy,
I was her boy, I was supposed to be her life support.

See, diabetes came callin,
God made his decision and there was no more stallin.
Kidney Dialysis, to leg amputations, it wasn't enough,
WHERE IS MY DAD...it's time for him to make me tuff.
When it comes to dating who will size her up like a mother should,
Because to a mothers son...no woman will ever be good.
But the foundation had been laid, she had to have prayed,
For my soul because my sisters are mothers, my wife is a mother,
My daughter will one day be a mother!
She knew! This wasn't a game to her,
She raised me to treat all these women the same as her.

Damn I miss my mother...
I want her to comeback and smother, me like a pork chop,
Her food was so good it can make a man heart stop.
As my emotions pull me in every direction,
I still look to her for protection,
I don't know rather to laugh, cry or pray...
All I know is that I want to give my mother a hug
On the second Sunday, in May."

Thoughts of a Foster Dad: Key Beliefs and Takeaways

- If family members were willing and able to step up and take care of kids in a moment of crisis, there'd be a lot less foster kids in the system.
- Every foster kid has experienced some type of trauma and loss. The sooner you can get that child support, the better. The more competent and caring people in their lives, the stronger their resilience will be. This is imperative for the healing process to occur.
- Foster kids generally want to do well. Ultimately, they want to make the ones that care for them happy.
- It is vital that foster children are encouraged to do something constructive that they like. Sports, clubs, hobbies, theater, music, dance...something. There are no labels in this area. To a foster kid, a playing field, in a controlled, safe, and learning environment, will be the most normal thing in his/her life. Outside of that, everything about that child's world is often labeled.
- Who do you know that is doing foster care? It takes a village. The village is the people that will help fill in the missing pieces necessary for survival for both the family and the child. My village just so happened to be my Aunt and Uncle, coaches, friends and their families. As a child, I was fortunate enough to have a strong support system.

Chapter 3: The Importance of Sports

Team sports help kids to be successful later in life by teaching them leadership and teamwork, healthy lifestyle, high self-esteem, providing educational benefits and teaching discipline, respect, and trust.

The summer before my mom passed away, sports became my biggest escape from dealing with my life at home.

I walked onto the baseball diamond at Mid-City Baseball and the GAP Baseball league down at Sheldon Field. Mr. Reuben Smartt knew me right away.

"Big Mack, this your boy Julian?" He shouted at my father.

"Yeah!" He replied prideful.

Mr. Smartt chuckled and answered, "That's a good looking kid, he must take after Dorothy?"

My Dad grinned and said, "You know it."

Finally talking to me, Mr. Smartt said "Goodson get out there and let's see what you got. What position can you play?"

"Second base," I said nervously.

Hand on his ball cap, bat in his hand, he asked, "Who is your favorite second baseman?"

"Sweet Lou Whitaker! I wanna be just like him," I said eagerly, waiting to rattle off stats if Mr. Smartt asked.

Mr. Smartt, hardly suppressing a smile with his salted goatee, said, "Grab your glove. Julian, this is Johnny. He'll play short. Greg will pitch. Lark will catch. Ricky will play third. You'll be tossing over to Jody...he's at first." He directed us all, pointing his bat at each position.

"Okay," I squawked excitedly.

Mr. Smartt gripped his big stick, a green Louisville Slugger that he called his Fungo. He screamed, "okay Goodson," and tapped a ground ball to me. I grounded it and threw it over to first. We repeated the process in similar form. Then he hit one harder and Mr. Smartt was starting to get a small sweaty lather built up. He said, "turn two" and blasted one to me. I took it on the short-hop, flipped the ball over to J-Walk at short and he threw a cannon over to Jody at first. I never saw a 13-year-old throw that hard. I could hear the ball buzzing through the air as it popped Jodi's first base mitt. I looked at him and nodded my approval. He looked at me and the chemistry between the two of us was born; I had my running mate.

A small crowd gathered around the fence – and that's when I saw him. He was loud, cocky and obnoxious! He stood tall and he stood out. I was paralyzed with fear because he was wearing a police uniform and the last time I had seen a policeman that close to my dad, he was handcuffing him, as he was face down on the floor. The officer at the fence was Maurice Barnes. My fears started to subside as he slapped my dad a high five. When I saw that Coach Barnes wasn't a threat to my dad, my anxiety level came down a couple hundred notches. Mo, our name for Coach Barnes, then very loudly told Mr. Smartt, "This whole infield will play for me!" That day I became a Seidman Tiger, but for me it was much bigger than making the team. It was the acceptance that I needed. Little did I know that Mo would go on to play a very important role for me as a black professional in the public eye.

After practice, everyone was congregating in the dugout.

"Y'all wanna go hoop? Ole Mo, can you handle the ball like you can pick it at second?" J-Walk said to me in a challenging tone.

"Yeah, I can play," I weakly uttered.

We ended up at Martin Luther King Park in southeast Grand Rapids. The place was a basketball mecca; it had five full court pick-up basketball games being played at any given time. My homeboy little Lee Figures was there. I slapped him a pound and then yelled, "Hey, he playing with us!"

After proving myself on the court amongst all of them, I was on cloud nine. A man approached me that I had never seen before and said, "Hey Goodson, come over here." I went, and he introduced himself as Mr. Foster.

"You Big Mack's kid right?" he asked, hands on his knees, bent over, sweating, and breathing hard.

"Yeah," I responded nervously.

Controlling his breathing, he said "I've been talking to your dad and he wants you to play for me."

"I'm already playing for the Seidman Tigers," I responded confusingly.

"Not baseball," he laughed. "Basketball. I just watched you play a couple of games. You can handle the ball out there. I want you to be my point guard. But a point guard has to be a leader. Are you a leader, Goodson?" He asked seriously.

"Yeah!" I responded in an attempt to add bass to my voice, poking my chest out.

By the end of that summer, I was riding my bike to baseball practice and then leaving that practice to go to basketball. The beauty of being on the field and being on the court is that it made me normal. It made me just one of the guys. There, my problems went away.

I didn't see police lights.

I didn't have any thoughts of a drug transaction.

My mom's sickness didn't exist.

On the field and on the court I was safe!

My coaches were two of the biggest community members and supporters of youth in the city. Maurice Barnes was the Youth Director of Seidman Center, a Boys and Girls Club. Bobby Foster was a mainstay at the Downtown YMCA as well as a coach for Grand Rapids Parks and Recreation. Both knew my dad well, respected him, and in many ways, looked up to him. Sports not only provided me safety but it kept me busy and out of harm's way while being in a challenging environment. Sports gave me structure, discipline, exercise, and guidance. My coaches were like father figures, teaching me life lessons through sports. At a time when my dad wasn't always present, my coaches were there for me. They would drop whatever they were doing to make sure that I was okay. Sports gave me a reason to want to do well in school. Anything lower than a 2.0 GPA and you were not allowed to play. No exceptions. Many of my friends would fall victim to this rule and have to sit out. Some of those same friends got into some serious trouble. I always wondered what would have happened to them if they had been able to play.

Spoken words of a Foster Dad

This poem was inspired by my friend, April of the YME...a stop the violence movement for the youth.

Just with him yesterday

I've had many friends that have touched my life in some way only to be put in jail or worse, put in a grave, did they deserve what they got for the way that they misbehaved. It's debatable, the greed we need is attainable, if I do this one lil thing...my dough will grow and my shine will be sustainable.

J-Walk – You was the smoothest dude on the baseball diamond, the skills you possess shoulda got you outta this mess so that you could afford to buy big diamonds, but you went left, when you shoulda steered right and that dream left when the Rover was pulled over on a street called Diamond. Damned rocks, my boy got popped and I think about you every time I watch the Red Sox. JBG the smoothest MC that never made it, and these thoughts blast their own music as the memories to your record is faded, it was in the cards and you played it. Won't let no one dis him I was just with him yesterday, and I already miss him.

Lee – You was the coolest dude at Alexander Elementary, before thoughts of death or the penitentiary, you wore high top Cons and Levi Jeans, the kid with swag really! I remember the kid that rounded third and slid into home, slappin high fives to his team, not what the news portrayed, as a gold chain wearin drug dealer that was slayed, at the age of seventeen. Fast money is relentless, instead of baseballs flying over fences, we got jail cells, caskets and violence that's senseless, that lavish lifestyle we seek leaves lives that are bleak, as loved ones suffer the consequences. Thoughts of you swell the eyes like onions, and I'll give anything to go with you and Buscat to Miss Tracy's for a bag of Funyons. Won't let no one dis him, I was just with him yesterday and I already miss him.

Greg – my boy playin shortstop, smallest dude with the biggest heart as he fielded the short hop. All city wrestler, people looked amazed as he pounced his guy, commanding attention, challenging the hood to a game of bounce and fly. To lose your life over dollars still makes no sense, poor life conditions got people dense, the happy hood just lost another Prince, lighters in the air every time I drive past your house on Prince. Won't let no one dis him, I was just with yesterday and I already miss him.

The moral of the story is this, there are many more that I could add to this list. Marcus, Val, Vontay, are friends that I miss. I feel blessed, it could have been me, did I make better choices, I don't know, I'd like to think so, but I still hear their voices. I wonder if they see me, with a wife, business owner, career, and a dad, I hope they are proud and glad that imma college grad. Their memories are inspirational, and because of them my goals are motivational.

Shout out to Mid-City, taught by leaders that are gritty, that gave us life lessons that showed no pity, producing strong character boys to men that need to step up and run the city. I won't let no one dis them, I was just with them yesterday and I already miss them.

Thoughts of a Foster Dad: Key Beliefs and Takeaways

- A foster kid wants to feel normal. Sports can provide normalcy – a place where a kid is not labeled.
- A foster kid will need a peer group. The guys that were on my sports teams became my friends. Some are still my friends today. All of my sons have developed healthy relationships from the sports teams that they've been a part of.
- Find a mentor for your foster kid. I was lucky to have not one but two very strong men that helped me along the way in the form of my coaches. A strong mentor will give your kid an outlet to talk and vent. My coaches helped me sidestep many of the pitfalls that my friends were unable to avoid.
- Sports, sports, and more sports! It is the best way to channel all of that pent up anger and aggression. Only on the playing field is it recommended and encouraged to hit something or someone as hard as you can and not get in trouble for it.
- Find positive outlets for your kids. Mine was sports and later it became writing and poetry. The poetry that I shared on social media, along with the likes and comments were validating and very therapeutic.
- Coaches, take your job seriously! As a youth, I didn't remember all of my teachers in school, but to this day, I remember every coach that I've ever had. Foster kids, especially, are constantly seeking positive affirmation and validation. As a coach, you can provide that. Coaches have the opportunity to change the trajectory of a child's life.

Chapter 4: Nineteen and Scared As Hell

Did you know?

Teenage girls that spend time in the foster care system are 57% more likely to become pregnant prior to their eighteenth birthday.

It had been my mom's dream for me to go to college and it became my aunt's goal to get me there after I moved in with her. I was all set to go to Ferris State University up in Big Rapids, Michigan until life happened.

"Julia Michelle Goodson born December 17, 1991, to Julian Goodson (Father, nineteen) and Janine Parker (Mother, seventeen)."

I met Janine at a house party right down the street from my house on Eastern Avenue in Southeast Grand Rapids. Ten months after meeting Janine, we were parents. Quite honestly, neither one of us knew what we were doing.

A week after we met, she invited me to her house on Prince Street and that's when I met her foster mom, Mary Adams. At this point, I had been introduced to adoption through my Aunt and Uncle who adopted my cousins Marcus and Ryan. I was also introduced to the concept of foster care indirectly by my Aunt and Uncle taking care of me and allowing me to live with them. Going to Janine's house; however, was the first time that I witnessed a foster home. From the outside looking in, I was being exposed to foster care. At Janine's house, I observed a foster home, a foster family, and the foster care system. My first impression was, "what the hell is this?" It was dysfunction at its finest. I counted four foster kids, one being Janine's infant, and three other girls. I also counted six biological kids. They were all living there in a three bedroom, one- and-a-half bath house, without a father-figure in sight.

Mary was really nice, she reminded me of Aunt Jemima, although a much skinnier version. She made me feel very comfortable, like I was family right off the bat. When she asked me where I was going to school and I said, "Ferris," she was visibly impressed. The biological siblings in the house ranged from twelve to early thirties. I instantly gravitated towards Jug, a fifteen-year-old going on twenty. He was a few years younger than me but he hung out with older kids at Ottawa Hills High School, so we had some mutual friends. Jug looked and acted like a young Will Smith in his Fresh Prince of Bel-Air days and everyone told him so. We became brothers right away.

The next time I went to Janine's house she was locked in her room, literally. There was a fight between one of the brothers and Janine was scared. During the fight, I saw who was in charge and it was most definitely Mary. When she talked everyone listened as she commanded their respect. I could feel something was off though. In the midst of all of this surfaced turmoil, I was asked to stay for dinner and nervously accepted. Before dinner Mary asked Jug to go upstairs and get the key to the pantry. This was extremely confusing to me.

Later that day, playing a game of Madden, I asked Jug, "Why do y'all lock up the food?" He responded, "Because one time, my mom went away for a night and when she came home all the food was gone. One of my brothers ate almost everything. The next day she put the whole house on a hunger strike."

"A hunger strike?" I asked.

He said, "Yeah she wouldn't let us eat for three days. Next time that happens I'm coming to your house."

I was floored. What he didn't tell me was that the person that ate all the food was his foster brother. He was hoarding and gorging food until Mary kicked him out for doing so.

I thought, "Maybe he was eating like that because he didn't know when he'd eat again." I decided to keep that thought to myself.

To this day, I am convinced that Mary was a foster parent for the money. To me, it seemed she thought, the more kids, the more money. However, she was a stickler for the rules and discipline; it was her way or the highway. Some of the things that I witnessed that brought me to this conclusion included her locking a six-year-old foster child in a closet for discipline, biological boys having sex with the foster girls, and a wooden spoon that she nick-named "Slappy Whappy." I knew Mary was a good person; she treated me like a son and I will be forever grateful for what she did for me. However, she fancied herself on being "Mother of the Century" and I always frowned upon it because of the stupidity that happened with her kids, in her house, on her watch. In my opinion, there was no way in hell should she have been a foster parent. Looking back on it, I could've made a phone call and reported things that I saw but I was only nineteen years old...what did I know?

I decided to go to Davenport College and not Ferris State University. Quite honestly, the university and dorm life intimidated me a little bit. I wasn't quite ready to be in a place where there was no family. I obtained my first apartment at Wingate in Kentwood. During Janine's pregnancy, we were still a couple. I had a full load of classes at Davenport while working two jobs, one at the bookstore as a work-study and another at Best Buy in Eastbrook Mall. Halfway through my second year at Davenport, I got mononucleosis.

The doctor told me, "Julian, you can work or go to school, but you can't do both or you will not get better."

I had a decision to make. When my daughter Julia was just born, Janine and I were on the outs. Let's just say I was coming into my own and started to explore other options. Teenagers with two kids trying to make it work like grownups...yeah right.

I went to Mary and told her what the doctor said. She scratched me a check that covered a semester of tuition and books. My Aunt Carol floated me some rent money and I continued to go to school. My grades were average but at least I was making progress. With a newborn, two jobs, and school, I thought I was doing fine especially since I never took out a student loan.

Looking back, Janine must have had a very good social worker at the time. At seventeen years old, she had two kids under the age of three and she was attending Park High School, an alternative school for pregnant girls and young mothers. Her social worker set her up with something she described to me as independent living. She moved out of Mary's house and was handed the keys to a furnished two-bedroom apartment on the northeast side of Grand Rapids. She had a new apartment, a cash assistance welfare stipend, over four hundred dollars a month in food stamps, with only an electric bill to pay – all paid for by the foster care system.

I remember asking myself, "how is this independent living when everything has been handed to you?"

It was kind of an oxymoron. At the time, we thought that she would be okay, that we would be okay. That was exactly what she needed. Being that I was a very young man at the time, I was confused and scared. I was sending her mixed messages. I was a boyfriend when I came over to see the kids, but when I left, I was single. In hindsight, it was the start of our break-up and a recipe for disaster. Given her situation, these are the barriers and situations that she had to overcome and deal with as a young mother:

- Two kids in diapers under the age of three
- Go to school with two kids, across town, catching two buses two hours one way
- Attend parenting classes
- Grocery shopping
- Cooking
- Cleaning
- Buying clothes, diapers, and food for two kids
- Depression

Honestly, we didn't stand a chance! I think the biggest reason for our demise was I was not allowed to move in with her. The agency had strict rules about boyfriends spending the night. We had a curfew and they monitored it. Had I moved in, I would've been able to help her with the day to day living that she struggled with. At a time when black fathers were increasingly absent in my community, here I was attempting to be present. Why weren't there services for the young men that wanted to be there for their children? In my opinion, it's still an under-served demographic to this day.

I would go over to Janine's house and it appeared like the life of a stereotypical welfare receiving, young, clueless mother. There were kids running around with dirty diapers, dirty dishes in the sink, overflowing trash, and no order whatsoever. It appeared to be complete and utter chaos. Seeing this is when the fighting and the bickering started. I blamed her for not being able to take care of simple things, like keeping house. I yelled at her, chastised her for not going to school. She dropped out of school and that's when I knew that I'd never be with her. I let her know about it every chance I got. Then, I did what most teenage boys would do, I left and did teenage things.

I was wrong. I was so wrong.

It wasn't Janine's fault. Janine came into the foster care system at fifteen-years-old with her older sister. The hand that she was dealt looked a little like this:

- Mom was a prostitute, addicted to crack-cocaine, and eventually married one of her jons before stealing from him and draining his life-savings
- Poverty – basic needs weren't met. Food, clothes, shelter affection, etc.
- Dad was mom's pimp
- Witnessed sexual abuse
- Witnessed drug abuse
- Physical abuse from grandparents
- Verbal and emotional abuse

This just scratched the surface of what Janine had to overcome and the daily torture that she had to live with. She was destined to be a third generation welfare recipient and she was perfectly ok with it because it was all that she knew. It wasn't her fault. Had Janine had more competent caring adults in her life, it would have increased her resiliency, which could have then led her on a different path.

For years, I "dogged" Janine out for being a deadbeat mom when in actuality, she was a victim of circumstance and her environment. Society expects people to pick themselves up by their bootstraps and dust themselves off. Society expects you to persevere through adversity. THAT'S BULLSHIT! Society expects all of this to occur, but doesn't understand that a person has to be taught how to overcome adversity.

I often find myself thinking, 'what if.' What if Janine just wasn't that strong? Or even worse, what if Janine was that strong but just didn't have the tools necessary to survive? What if she had a support system to simply show her how? What if the foster home that Janine landed at would have been ideal for her instead of a chaotic mess? What if her Aunt, who seemed to be a stable woman, would have taken her in?

And then one day it happened.

I went to pick my daughter Julia up for a visit. Janine was happy for me to come get her and give her a break. When I arrived to the small duplex on Griggs street on the southeast side of Grand Rapids, the place was a train wreck. It looked like she had a party the night before. Julia's 3-year-old brother was pouring himself a bowl of cereal. The place reeked of stale cigarette smoke, weed, and dried up alcohol in the carpet. Empty Old E 40 ounce bottles were everywhere. Packs of Philly Blunts and Swisher Sweet boxes were on the table and the floors. There was a man that I had never seen before snoring on the couch. The kids were happy to see me. Julia was crawling around on the dirty floor. From the kitchen, I saw a small mouse dart out from behind the refrigerator and dive into a register vent. I picked up Julia off the floor. She was wearing pajamas with the feet in them. She was dirty, she smelled, and her diaper needed to be changed. Her hair was nappy and in desperate need of a comb, a hot one! My blood was boiling. My first inkling was to go off on Janine, but I chilled and played it cool. I just wanted to get my daughter out of there. I walked out with Julia on my hip and Janine said, "You're forgetting the diaper bag."

I hollered back, "I'm good, we don't need it." Seeing that mouse, and those conditions of Janine's house was an extreme trigger for me, one like you wouldn't believe. I strapped Julia in the car seat and drove off.

I never took her back.

I took Julia back to my apartment, cleaned her up, put some new clothes on her and made spaghetti with pineapple on the side for dinner. She ate and she ate and she ate some more. She just kept eating. She polished off a whole can of pineapples and a plate of spaghetti. I thought, "Wow she has a healthy appetite for a two-year-old!" That's when I realized that she was hungry. She ate like she didn't know when she would eat again. I went to the bedroom and shed a tear. Up until then, I had only seen Julia sparingly over the first year and a half of her life. I was so busy working, going to school, and being a bachelor that I was not being a father. That day, I decided that I would be the best father I could be. In doing so, and making that decision, she had to be with me. I could be a much better father to her if she woke up under the same roof as me.

But her hair. What was I supposed to do about her hair?

We got in the car and went over to my sister, Tracey's house.

I said, "Tracey, will you please braid Julia's hair with the pretty beads in it. You know, the kind of french-braided hairstyle that I don't have to worry about for a couple weeks?"

"Yeah" she replied with the biggest grin on her face. "She looks just like her big cousin AJ" she continued, comparing my daughter to her own.

I told Tracey I'd be right back as it had just dawned on me that I didn't have a diaper bag. I went to the store and bought everything she needed. Diaper bag, diapers, more clothes, wipes, baby powder, lotion, and bed sheets just to get started. I looked up and the bill totaled a little over $300. When I got back to Tracey's house, she helped me assemble the diaper bag and asked, "Ole...where did you get all this money from?"

That's when it hit me – I had just spent all of the rent money on my daughter. I was completely in over my head. I was a twenty-one-year-old single black man with a two-year-old daughter. That was the day I went from being a father to being a dad. I wasn't a "baby daddy" anymore. I was scared as hell, but I had an unrecognizable confidence. I couldn't show fear in front of my daughter. Up until then, I didn't have one male friend that had ever taken custody of their child. It seemed I was a rare breed. At that moment, my life changed again, and I knew that I would spend the rest of my life protecting my kid.

Spoken words of a Foster Dad

My daughter is graduating from high school in May! Anyone that has a child can understand the pride and joy that comes with such a milestone...this is what came out! Shout out to my friend Shanato for the title!

It Began

It began when I got custody of you when you were two years old. A female mini me, your mom wasn't the enemy, as it was my pleasure to treasure you like gold.

It began at Meijer with a pony ride. You yanked my arm outta my socket, as you demanded all of the change in my pocket. Your style is perfect, I made sacrifices but you were worth it. Your brightness stretched for many miles, and these pennies... I made sure I had plenty, bought us many smiles.

It began with your first bike as I taught you how to ride, our happiness we couldn't hide. I knew you were a tuffy, when you skinned your knee from falling off of your pink Huffy. You said "Dad this time go slow." "I will," I said, "I won't lose sight, I'll run alongside of you and hold on tight, I promise I won't let go."

It began in middle school when you made the cheer team, watching you scream, jump, kick, and yell, you made my eyes swell, and my pride beam, doing back flips and I knew I saw it all when you dropped and did the splits.

It began when I took you and that boy on your first date. I wasn't naggin, I just didn't like the way his pants was saggin. You said, "Don't embarrass me" you begged me, but I couldn't help it, thoughts edgy, so I walked behind him and gave him a wedgy...the look in your eye, I know you wanted to die. :-)

It began when you moved out to Arizona. It was devastating to both of us as the days were long and the nights were longer, and although we didn't see each other that much, and we couldn't touch, our bond became stronger. Tears in your eyes as you start to stutter, as I manage to utter, Julia...take care of your little brother.

It began as a little girl and you blossomed into a beautiful young woman, and nothing will stop the tears from comin. So you no longer have to use your imagination, the gateway to adulthood is here and it began with your high school graduation.

There will be no endings, many more milestones are blessings in the form of your career, a wedding day, and your own children. So it will begin, it will begin, it will begin...this is just one chapter and it

doesn't have to end.

Thoughts of a Foster Dad: Key Beliefs and Takeaways

- Teenagers are kids, too! Just because Janine was a mother and had her own apartment, didn't mean that she all of a sudden had become an adult. She was still very much a kid, with no idea as to how to take care of herself.
- Social workers – please screen your clients. Make sure that the youth you are working with are mature enough to handle living on their own. Even if they are mature enough, they still need guidance, support and resources to help them succeed. I understand that sometimes you have dire circumstances, but teenagers need to have a basic understanding of sustainable living skills.
- Bad placements. Sometimes you will have a placement that is not a good fit. The screening process of accepting a placement can be rushed made out of desperation. Try to get as much information as possible, so that you are able to make an informed decision.
- Because the screening process needs to be tightened up, kids are set up to be independent before they are ready, as was the case with Janine. She would have been better off in some form of a mentor situation prior to moving out on her own.
- When a teen-mother and her child come into care, investigate the role of the father. In my situation, no one ever asked me "Hey, where are you? How can you help?" or "What can we do to help you be a father and provide for your child?"

Chapter 5: Trauma - Poetry in Motion

100% of all children that have spent time in the foster care system have experienced trauma.

Phoenix, Arizona May, 2009

It was eight o'clock at night and the heat was in the triple digits. It was hot! My one-bedroom apartment overlooking Glendale Mall in West Phoenix was boiling and so was my attitude. I had just got off the phone with my ex-wife Mandy, the mother of my eight-year-old son Gunnor and adoptive parent of my now seventeen-year-old daughter Julia. Mandy had just hung up on me after a completely one-sided conversation.

"Mandy all I want to do is see my kids." I screamed angrily into the phone.

"We had plans and it's not your night." She barks back.

"But Julia called and asked me to come and pick her and her brother up. It didn't sound like you had plans. She said you didn't." I pleaded.

"I don't owe you an explanation." She barked back.

"Seriously? I moved three thousand miles away from my home so that I could have a more active role in my kid's lives. I'm trying to be much more than just a part-time dad," I shouted, still angry.

"You should've thought of that when you abandoned us for another woman," she screamed into the phone.

"Mandy that was five years ago. By us not getting along, we are only hurting the kids. Why won't you let me see them more?" I said in an exhausted tone.

"Because I don't have to," she says, through clenched teeth.

I growled "YOU ARE SUCH A BITCH!!!!" She hung up the phone.

I was as heated as the Phoenix asphalt pavement at three o'clock in the afternoon in the middle of June. I was alone in a very big city. No family and only few friends, none of whom knew my situation, my story, or my struggle. It was very difficult for me to talk to my then wife Stephanie about the situation because she felt that I abandoned her and her two kids to move there.

Realizing how alone I was, I started shaking uncontrollably and lost my breath. I was having the first of many panic attacks. Once it subsided a little, I called my old boss, Todd back in Grand Rapids, and asked him to help me with some counseling. I needed to talk to someone and it should probably be a professional. I felt as if I was about to die. He put me in touch with a family support 24 hour hotline.

I dialed the phone with nothing to lose. The lady on the other end helped me with my breathing and told me to imagine a pizza. She told me to imagine the best pizza that I'd ever had in my life and breathe it in as deep as I could. I thought this lady was crazy and I was unable to do it at first. The second time I breathed it in, I could feel my heart rate going down. The third breath took me back to Burton and Kalamazoo Street in Grand Rapids Michigan. I closed my eyes and imagined I was inside Mineo's Pizza House. I smelled the pizza. Now I was salivating.

I can't believe that it worked.

After she got me to calm down, she asked me some basic questions. She set up an appointment for me to meet with a therapist the next morning. It was a Friday night, so luckily I didn't have to go to work the next morning.

She said, "Julian, I want you to write down your thoughts on paper so that the therapist has a baseline for discussion."

I said, "OK" and hung up the phone.

As I hung up, I was still on edge. On the television was an HBO Special called 'Brave New Voices.' BNV was a poetry slam competition from youth all over the country. It was a spin-off show from Russell Simmons' show, *Def Poetry*. I sat down at the dining room table in the hot apartment with the air conditioner on full blast and started writing. Then I wrote some more. Then I cracked open a beer and wrote some more. Then I ordered a pizza and I wrote some more. Then I stretched out and did twenty push-ups, sat back down and wrote some more. I looked up. It was morning and the sun was coming up. The birds were chirping but I just wrote and wrote and wrote! I finally reread my work and started to cry. Anger, passion, frustration, regret, love, simplicity, complications, mystery, hurt, aggression, children, all came out at the same time. I had written fourteen poems in ten hours. It had all poured out of me. Every poem reflected on personal trauma from some point in my life that I had never dealt with. I read it again and cried some more. Not because I was happy or sad but because I was free. It was like God, Himself, gave me a new toy on Christmas morning.

None of the poems I wrote were good enough to win a Pulitzer. However, I had listened to enough bad rap music to know that it was better than a lot of garbage I had heard on the radio. It was a lot more complex and more creative than, "Roses are Red and Violets are Blue." It had substance, feeling, meaning, and passion. But most of all, it was me. These creative writings were my stories.

My phone rang and it startled me! Who was calling me this early? I answered. It was the therapist that I was scheduled to see. My appointment was set for eight o'clock in the morning. It now was a quarter after nine. I had missed it. She asked me if I was ok. I explained that I was up all night writing, that I hadn't slept. She asked me if I wanted to reschedule, but I simply told her no. She asked if I was sure and I responded by thanking her. When she told me to write down what I was feeling, it changed my life. It set me free. It unleashed a creative side of me that I didn't know existed. All of a sudden, it was like an eye doctor gave me the perfect prescription that allowed me to see life. But most importantly, writing gave me a coping skill. I never went to the counseling appointment. The pen was the best therapist I've ever had. I was armed with a weapon to combat my sadness, fight my stress, and slug my pain. It came in the form of a pen. It was Mother's Day weekend and I was in Phoenix alone. I didn't leave the apartment all weekend. I just wrote. Monday morning came around. It was time for me to share something that I wrote. It was as if I had this new found talent that I wanted to share with everyone.

Foster Care and Trauma

At this point you're probably asking yourself, what does this have to do with trauma and foster care? The answer is everything! All fourteen poems that I wrote dealt with a traumatic experience that occurred in my life. Up until that moment, I had never properly dealt with any of the loss or trauma. I never unpacked the shitty-life-hand that I was dealt. Every foster kid has experienced trauma.

What I started that hot night in Phoenix was what some therapists call the trauma narrative. When I started to share my story with the world, I received validation and positive attention from those that read my poem "Part Time Dad" (see below). However, I received much more than that; I came to the realization that I wasn't alone anymore. Even though I was in a big city foreign to me, I wasn't alone. There were a lot of people that were feeling what I was feeling; feeling my pain, sadness and mental anguish I had carried by myself for years. That day I received seventeen phone calls from five different states. I was reminded that I had friends and, because of my new-found talent, I had fans.

I turned my deepest pain into positive gain. I received messages from people that I didn't even know thanking me for what I wrote. Friends were encouraging me to keep my head up and to write more. The phone calls were so important. But none more important than Keith who was in California, Swell Nel in Georgia, and Buster and Greg in Michigan. They knew me, the real me. Their phone calls didn't surprise me, but their encouraging words of my new-found skill did. They were all shocked that I had it in me but they all told me it was good. I respected and valued their opinions. It made me feel good. It gave me purpose. They encouraged me to keep writing and keep sharing my stories.

What does this have to do with Adoption?

My daughter Julia was adopted by my ex-wife Mandy two years after we were married. Upon our divorce, we shared joint custody with Mandy being the custodial parent. Mandy petitioned the courts to move with Julia and my son, Gunnor, to Phoenix, Arizona. In court, my lawyer argued the family and fatherly bond that I had with my children was strong, and that the original court order should remain in place. Especially in the case of Julia. He argued that as the biological father, it was important that she remain in my care. The Judge had different thoughts. Once adopted there was a new birth certificate that was issued with Mandy's name on it. In the court of law, Mandy is her mom. The fact that she didn't birth Julia carried no weight. Mandy won her petition to move. I was devastated! The morning after the court's decision, my children moved abruptly to Phoenix, giving me about ten minutes to say goodbyes. It was at that moment that I fully understood the power of adoption.

When a parent loses their parental rights and their child is adopted by another family, there is a shift that takes place. The shift has everything to do with the adoptive parents. These adoptive parents matter more than anything or anyone, including biological parents. Believing that marriage was forever, I made the choice to have Mandy adopt Julia. When that happened, Janine didn't matter anymore. Janine was out of sight, out of mind in the eyes of Mandy and I. Besides, Mandy was the only mom that Julia knew. Even in divorce, Mandy still had the mentality that Julia was hers. Mandy believed that she had just as much, if not more rights than I did. And in the sight of the court, she was right!

Mandy also had ammunition. I was fired from a decent paying position at Pepsi Bottling Group for insubordination. In a year and half stretch, I racked up close to sixteen thousand dollars in back child support. I received a recommendation from the Friend of the Court (FOC) to cut my support payments in half, based on my decreased income. The Referee denied the recommendation and in doing so told me the following:

"Mr. Goodson you are college educated with experience. You are fully capable of paying the original order."

Six months later there was a bench warrant out for my arrest for failure to pay child support and I was arrested during a routine traffic stop. I bonded out and when I got home, I opened the mail and saw a foreclosure letter on my home. When it rains it pours. Damn adjustable rate mortgage. What was my realtor thinking? Along with the bad news from the mortgage company, I also noticed another letter from the FOC. The courts were suspending my driver's license for failure to pay child support. Try and make that make sense.

But there was the sunshine in my cloudy forecast, or so it appeared. I receive a call that could change everything. It was a job offer from Faygo Bottling Company with forty thousand dollars a year plus commission, company vehicle, cell phone, laptop, and benefits, etc. The offer was contingent upon passing a background check, including having a valid driver's license. HOLY SHIT! I immediately called FOC and told them that I had a job offer on the table.

"What can I do to get my license back?" I asked

Their response was for me to pay two months' worth of child support payments and my driver responsibility fees. It was a reinstatement fee totaling a little over two thousand dollars. The other option was to get my ex-wife Mandy to forgive some of my back support. After that, they could reinstate my license.

So, I asked Mandy to help me out, not only me but for her children, our children. She stood to gain eight hundred dollars a month with me taking that job. Without even thinking about it, she said, "No! I don't need the money that bad."

"What the fuck," I thought! "Did she really just turn down eight hundred dollars a month? Did she really just turn down an opportunity for her children's father to become gainfully employed?" The courts could care less that I was a good dad because all they cared about was the money and the lack of funds that FOC received.

While in court battling for custody, Mandy's lawyer argued that I was a deadbeat and my entire character was called into question by a man being paid to discredit me. I felt that my soul was being judged by a Referee in a robe that didn't know me and never met me. Mandy's lawyer also argued that she was receiving a significant raise from a job that she was to receive if she was able to leave. Four hours later the Referee slammed her gavel and ruled in Mandy's favor. FOUR HOURS! Four hours was all it took for my life to be changed as I knew it. The fate of Julia and Gunnor's relationship with their dad was determined in only four hours. The Faygo job offer was never brought up in court. Up until I was fired from Pepsi I was current on my child support payments. Before I knew what hit me, Mandy, Julia, and Gunnor left for Phoenix. I was crushed. I later learned in therapy, that the loss of my children in them moving across the country was traumatic. No sooner than I learned what I was going through, I immediately thought of my kids. What did their trauma triggers look like in this matter? They were equally affected. When I called Mandy to explain to her what could be happening to our children, she laughed at the thought. They never received counseling while in Phoenix.

Losing a court battle and watching your children move across the country is a very traumatic experience. It is still difficult for me to deal with it years later. "Julian I am going to hit you where it hurts the most...I'm going to hit you in the pocket and good luck seeing your kids." Mandy actually said that and boy did she mean it. I am not proud of what I did and how I hurt her. I did some things that I wish I could take back. But I thought she wouldn't keep the kids away from their dad to spite me. Ultimately, hurting them....would she? Uhhh, yes!!!! The court order allowed visitation every Wednesday from five o'clock pm to eight o'clock pm and every other weekend. Mandy followed the court order to the letter. She didn't allow me to see Julia and Gunnor any other time than what the order said. One day I got out of work early and went to daycare to pick up my son at about three o'clock in the afternoon. We were so happy to see each other until the daycare came and said "I'm sorry Julian, but we can't let you take Gunnor until five o'clock tonight." His daycare teacher then proceeded to take out a court order that Mandy provided for them and show it to me. Gunnor began to cry hysterically and, at that point, I was convinced that she was the most spiteful woman on the planet. The answer to my question was yes...yes she would hurt her children to spite me. To this day, Mandy and I don't speak.

When dealing with trauma, the average person has a hard enough time overcoming what we've been through. Navigating the waters of something that has been life altering can set your sails off course. Some people never get back on course and deal with it. Many people mask the pain. They turn to alcohol or drugs while some turn to promiscuity or many other forms of harmful self-inflicting behavior. As it pertains to kids in foster care, it is much worse and could be detrimental to development. Not dealing with traumatic experiences can cause future relationship problems. It will be very hard for kids to trust and connect to others. In hindsight, I believe this was the case for me.

When a foster kid comes into my home, I truly believe that my wife and I are fully equipped to help provide this kid with a stable life. My wife and I have been through countless hours of trauma training; in addition, my traumatic experiences as a young black teenage male prepared me to handle a multitude of different situations scenarios and expectations.

Neglect - I went through it.

Abuse - I went through it.

Lack of food and being hungry - I went through it.

Losing a loved one - I went through it.

Seeing your friends killed - I went through it.

Watching your friends get arrested - I went through it.

Watching your dad get arrested - I went through it.

Because of these experiences, I feel equipped to talk to a kid about his situation. Now granted, there are a lot of extremes and every child is different. As a foster dad, it is my job to notice and recognize what's going on with kids emotionally. I have the ability to pay attention to the signs and triggers that a child will show you.

Spoken words of a Foster Dad

For years, I lived in Grand Rapids Michigan. My kids lived in Phoenix Arizona. I only saw them when they weren't in school. It equaled out to be a little over nine weeks a year. According to the new court order, after Mandy was allowed to leave, I was allowed: six weeks in the summer, a week at spring break, and eleven days at Christmas. This small amount of time made me feel like a part-time dad. I hated it!

This is for everyone with children!

Part-Time Dad

I remember when my son was born. I promised myself that I would be the best father I could be. His mom and I are starting a new chapter, one with joy and laughter, because now we have a baby to look after. Months go by and the stresses of life cause me to stray, cause no matter how hard I pray, forever with his mom wasn't happening anyway. So I bounced, and I made a big mistake that day.

Now I'm dealing with a woman scorned, determined to make a man mourn, damn I wish my father was there to warn. When I left, in her eyes I went from father to baby daddy. I'm a good father but only from 5 to 8 on Wednesday when I have money to spend, and maybe every other weekend. See baby daddy's don't get excited, about a birthday because they ain't invited. You're on her shit-list, so you can forget about Christmas, because to you, Jesus was born on December 26th.

Not to mention the FOC. You know, Forgetting Our Children. See my wife loses respect when I go to the mailbox and there is half of a check, so sometimes my life is a complete wreck. You can't put a price tag on a dad! You can't put a price tag on being a dad! A father realizes self-worth, so he helps his daughter with her homework. A father realizes that his son can sway, so he teaches him how to dribble a ball in the driveway.

So when I walk into the Forgetting Our Children (FOC) office to be judged by a lady that don't know me, my head is held high because my balance is current, respect is what they owe me. So women, if you got a real man but he keep coming up short don't get mad, please keep his children in his life, a real man is never a part-time dad!

Spoken words of a Foster Dad

My father recently lost his long battle with Parkinson's disease. I'm grieving now and this is what came out! This is for anyone that has ever lost a parent...

BE HAPPY FOR ME!

As a young boy I would ask my father, where are you going and he would tell me "down the road of peace!" That was his subtle way of telling me to mind my own business. My family and friends have all witnessed, me living life to the fullest, I've had a good life; however, I'm going someplace better than this. So be happy for me! Dad where you going? To hell if I don't pray! Where I'm going the sky is not Grey, my spirit is protected, keeping the devil away.

Be happy for me! I'm a smoke good where I'm going and I don't have to worry about the "Greens"! For those that don't know, that's the collards, cash flow and the well... you know! Be happy for me! My soul has been prayed for and I know that I'm worthy, it's time for me to click my heels 3x's because I'm going home to Dorothy.

Be happy for me! Where I'm going I'll be sportin my Bally Suit while standing tall with my 6ft 5in chocolate frame, and everyone will still know my name, working the room with my charm, but my smile is much wider now because my wife is on my arm. Be happy for me! Tonight I hit the 4 digit when 1010 was played, so we having a party and everyone is invited to play bridge, dominoes and spades.

Be happy for me! There are no more shakes and I got ribs and steaks, it's the 4th of July and I'm takin the whole neighborhood to Gun Lake. Be happy for me! The only "PARK-IN-MY-SON is Derek in the blue convertible takin everyone to Johnson Park, my world is no longer darker, I'm going home...and I'm taking everyone a burger from Parkers. Mack Henry Goodson...there will never be another, on Sunday I'm going to the Fanitorium to throw strikes with my brother. Be happy for me! My body may be gone but my soul is not deceased, I've traveled down many roads in my life and I have finally found my peace

Many kids lose parents every day! Foster kids, however, are going through a multitude of different traumas. Let's say a fourteen year old kid's mom dies and there isn't a viable option for that child to have a family member to look after them. That kid is then removed from the home that he is in and may be placed in an emergency shelter facility, if there aren't any available foster homes that are willing to care for a teenage boy. That kid is now going through two different types of trauma at the same time.

> A) The devastation and grief of losing a parent.

> B) The terrifying circumstances and fear that come from being removed from his home.

There's a really good chance that a kid can end up in a residential facility where he would then be subjected to other kids such as him, all with horrifying issues. All living under one roof. For some, its sink or swim, fight or flight, life or death. Luckily for me, I had family that was there but it took two years for me to find stability. I never had a grief counselor talk to me once. No one at Ottawa Hills High School ever asked me how I was doing outside of my immediate friends. No school counselor knew of my situation and talked to me about services that they could provide, if any. Coaches assumed that I was good because I appeared strong on the outside and normal on the playing field. Many times, when kids end up in a residential facility, they will receive therapy of some sort. However with me, I received nothing. That hot day in May when I decided to write is when my therapy began. Almost thirty years after my first recognizable traumatic experience when my house was raided! Posting it on social media started the dialogue where, "Likes" became a listening ear and "Comments" became very therapeutic with encouraging words like, "keep your head up" and "stay strong." Now as a foster dad my "Spidey Senses" are on high alert when one of my kids post something. I notice any and everything that's out of sorts on social media. As a foster dad and a parent for that matter, I am thankful for social media. There is a lot of usable information just from simply paying attention to what your kids post.

Thoughts of a Foster Dad: Key Beliefs and Takeaways

- Learn as much as you can about trauma. Learn about what triggers the traumatic memories for your child. For example, losing parents is a traumatic experience. If a child tells you that he is fine, trust me, he isn't.

- Trauma experts call what I experienced that day in my hot apartment as a "trauma narrative." It is defined as: "People who are exposed to traumatic events have a profound need to make sense of them. Survivors of trauma may require professional support to help them do so. Since survivors often find post-trauma thoughts and memories difficult to tolerate, therapy can provide a variety of techniques for coping on a daily basis. Telling the trauma story is one of the most effective coping strategies for dealing with trauma-related distress. Talking about a traumatic experience helps organize memories and feelings into a more manageable and understandable psychological 'package'. Telling the story, or developing a trauma narrative, is a significant step in the trauma recovery process no matter what array of symptoms is present." [http://www.ptsdtraumatreatment.org/the-trauma-narrative/]

- Encourage foster kids to indulge in something creative. Poetry, music and lyrics, blogging, writing, and journaling, theater, art, video production just to name a few. Typically, this will help some of what they went through to be expressed in a positive and constructive way.

Not only do foster kids carry baggage, foster parents do, too. Foster parents also carry their experiences from prior to the child moving into their home, the same as the kids do. It's important to recognize and own what you can so you can best help your kid work through theirs.

Chapter 6: Abandonment

It is my strong belief that one hundred percent of children in the foster care system will struggle with issues from abandonment.

"46% of all kids in foster care are placed in non-relative homes."

For many children, this may feel like the ultimate abandonment.

Did you know?

According to Webster's Dictionary:

Abandonment

Abandon

[uh-ban-dun n]

Verb (used with object)

1. *To leave completely and finally; forsake utterly; desert: "to abandon ones farm; to abandon a child; to abandon a sinking ship."*
2. *to give up; discontinue; withdraw from:*

Let me start out by saying that my father "Mack" Henry Goodson was an awesome man. He raised all four of us the best that he could. Some of his parenting traits echo in my relationships with my children. He had more people that loved and adored him than those that disliked him. However, there was a noticeable gap in his presence in my life. For a four-year stretch, beginning when the time I was fourteen years old until I turned eighteen, he was hardly around. And when he was present, he wasn't; he was physically there, but not in the moment. He was exercising his own demons from a substance abuse problem and I had to witness him fight this addiction. I had to watch him fight his losses. I had to watch him fight his personal shortcomings as a man. He fought a battle with his pride and lost. It was as if his nightmare never ended. He had just lost his wife, his better half, the glue that kept the family together. He was grieving the loss of his best friend. Before he died, I had to have a man-to-man talk with him and verbally forgive him. I was angry with him for not being there for me when I needed him most. Because even though he lost his wife, I lost my mom and he was the adult while I was just a child. I had to let him know how him not being present in those years affected me. I honestly believe the four year daddy gap has had a ripple effect on my relationships with Julia and Gunnor, Not once during this four-year stretch did he hug me and tell me, and say "everything will be okay." And boy, did I need him to.

Our relationship, as I grew up and became a man, was awesome. Our bond became very strong. As I matured, I could talk to him and ask him candid questions. It seemed like it was easier for him to be a parent to me as I became older. He didn't understand the nurturing part of being a parent when I was a teenager. However, he was who I learned from, who I wanted to be with. Had my dad been present, I would never have wanted to go to my Aunt's house. He was my first choice. The good, the bad, and the in-between, he was my first choice. I loved him with everything I had. I loved all of him including his flaws and I'd give anything to have a conversation with him right now.

When my mom died I felt abandoned by her. I was the youngest of four. My older sisters and brothers had other responsibilities and children. They had their own lives to lead and, although they were all there for me, I still felt abandoned by them. My older brother Derek and his wife Gwen took me in for a short stint but I felt as if I were a burden. They were newlyweds starting their family; in my mind, I didn't fit in. I was constantly distracted because I didn't fit in and I was always in the way. With all of that, I still was lost in a sea of people that looked just like me. Besides, Derek was my big brother. He didn't try to replace my dad. He stayed in his lane and remained a big brother when what I needed was my dad and what I craved was my mom. Although I had a support system, I was still very alone.

So, if I felt like that, even after moving in with my aunt and uncle, imagine a foster kid that doesn't know the people that they are forced to be a family with. How alone might this kid feel? Often, foster kids don't have the luxury of close family. If a parent dies, goes to prison, or is forced out of their lives some other way, they could end up in a group home setting. Ideally, a family member would intervene and take the child in to avoid all of that. If more family members were able and willing to step up, there'd be a lot less foster kids in the world.

A foster kid suffering from abandonment may also have some serious attachment issues. It will be hard for him to make and keep friends because of the lack of trust that they have. This may carry on into adulthood. It may be more difficult to sustain long-term relationships and even marriage. Often, foster kids don't even understand what they are going through. You can sometimes find the same traits in kids that come from single mother situations and may feel abandoned by their fathers. Foster kids move into a home with people that can be from different cultures and backgrounds. Getting comfortable with their surroundings will be hard enough. Add on feelings of abandonment, and it becomes extremely difficult for some foster kids to attach to a caregiver. The feeling of being alone or feeling like they have no one is real; although, they may have their basic needs met. They may have love, and nurturing, and safety, and still feel empty inside. A foster kid can walk in a crowded room and still feel alone.

Spoken words of a Foster Dad

ABANDONMENT

My definition of abandonment is when you are left by the people that you need the most, I'm scared, and don't want to get burnt like toast, my mom and dad has up and disappeared like ghosts. I'm 14 years old now, mom is gone; Dad, I need you now more than ever, but you're fighting your own demons as our tie starts to sever.

Mom gave me my foundation, to handle many situations, my mind is strong, don't need muscle, although you taught me to tussle...as you came thru with pounds of weed, that people need, sub-consciously showing me how to hustle. You did teach me not to hide, how to provide, you made me go to school, educated people rule, and for that I give thanks, but a teenage boy needs his dad, not police lights and holding tanks.

I never told you, but sometimes it didn't feel like I've ever really known you... I need something to ease the pain too, not drugs, didn't want to be like you, I want someone to show me love, so I guess these girls will have to do. Never got too close, never wanted to boast, numb when I'm with them as my feelings starts to coast. Can't let people in, that never paid dividends, parasites suck the life outta you, then they abandon again, not suicidal but I want this trend to end.

Mom since you left, I have nothing left, I keep turning left, ending up back where I started... I keep going left. To the right to the right, it doesn't have to be spite, everything that I need is in sight, if I keep it to the write to the write... Stop feeling sorry for yourself...you can do it, the seeds of my life was planted by my parents and they grew it, so I pretended to be strong and nobody knew it, as I abandon my own responsibilities...damn I blew it!

Now I'm a grown man, and still trying to understand, that kids emulate their parents, so I must have a better plan. My soul is still reeling, as I fight off the negative feelings. It's time to remove the black cloud, the storm has been lifted, and basking in the sun is your son who's warm and gifted. I got goals and causes to believe in, so therefore, I'm all done grievin, even on an autumn day I'm not leavin.

Forgiveness is in my heart now, giving my family a strong foundation to stand on, the ultimate love feeling has landed, learning from my sins, and never again, taking my family for granted, leave them stranded, leave them abandoned. My responsibilities of focus is concrete strong as I heel and repent, much time will be spent, so we don't ever have to suffer abandonment.

Thoughts of a Foster Dad: Key Beliefs and Takeaways

- Abandonment issues have a profound effect, even into adulthood.
- Every kid that comes into the foster care system might have at least some type of abandonment issues and/or struggles. Validating their feelings about their family without bashing their biological parents will help them process things in a healthy way.
- Many foster kids have no father in their lives and often don't know who their biological father is. Imagine looking in the mirror and not knowing who you are supposed to look like when you get older. Even if they have had a strong male role model in their lives such as a foster dad, step-dad or an uncle, they may still struggle with abandonment issues and an unhealthy hatred for the man that was supposed to be there and wasn't.
- The best thing you can do is deal with the problem head on. Address it. Acknowledge it. Validate it. Talk about it if they are open and ready for it. Get them counseling. All you can do as foster parents is model what parents are supposed to look like.
- Even as adults, some of us are dealing with 'daddy issues.' It will affect how you parent a child, especially a foster child.
- Authors, Dawn Walker and Matt Haviland, wrote a book called, "*The Daddy Gap*." The book does a good job of explaining the pitfalls that a child can fall into when a dad isn't present. Physically, my father was present. However, there was a four-year stretch after my mom died that my dad wasn't there. Physically, spiritually, or emotionally he was unavailable. I believe that, The "*Daddy Gap*" came into play for me. Fourteen to eighteen years old in a young man's life are very pliable years of development. I'm quite sure some decisions and behaviors that I displayed as a young

adult had to do with the lack of my father's involvement during my teenage years.

Chapter 7

Divorce. The Good, the Bad, the Ugly

"Nothing has prepared me more for being
a foster dad than going through a divorce."
~ Julian Goodson

The Good

One wouldn't think that any good could come out of a divorce. Divorce has to be one of the most painful experiences anyone could endure. I've been divorced twice now. I've experienced my fair share of heartache. However, I can say that nothing has prepared me more for being a foster dad than going through a divorce.

A man going through a divorce when there are kids involved has something to prove to almost everyone. He has something to prove to his soon-to-be ex-wife, her friends and family, his friends and family, the lawyers, Friend of the Court, the judge, his kids, but most importantly, himself.

"I am a good dad," he'll tell himself over and over and over, again and again.

"What makes a good dad?" He may say to himself, "A provider. A protector."

He'll get the kids on his weekend and it'll be instant fun. Movies, go-carts, festivals, dining out, seeing the town, and the list goes on and on. A divorced man's parenting style often suddenly overcompensates for his lack of being around. It's not that he is trying to win his kids over with what he can do for them or how much fun they can have, although some do. It's all about keeping the kids occupied. To this point, he's had help with day-to-day things, but now that help is no longer there. Eventually the fun events become expected, not only by the dad but by his kids.

Once a divorce evolves through its cycle, he then finds himself in unchartered waters. If the divorcee is smart, he'll figure out the fun events have to stop before his pockets are empty or his patience is worn. He'll figure out that it's not about what he can buy or the things he can say they did, it's about the quality time spent with his child(ren) and about getting to know them. It's about recognizing when they need a hug instead of a stern hand. It's about paying attention to his surroundings as well as theirs.

I became much more in tune with my children after my divorce than I was when I was with their mom. When a man is thrust into the caregiver role without a spouse involved, he begins to take on a role of "Super-Dad" with feelings. He can't simply say to a child in tears, "go see your mom." He is forced to deal with problems and handle it them the best way he knows how.

Divorce was an adjustment because I was trying to prove to everyone involved that I was who I thought I was. I learned how to get in tune with my children on a much deeper level.

What are they thinking?

What are they doing?

How can I help?

What would their mom do?

Naturally, most men want to "fix" problems. Going through a divorce forced me to become more attentive, alert, and most importantly, nurturing. I had to play more than one role because I couldn't call their mom and ask for help. In doing so, I gained a deeper appreciation for the role of a mother. I also had to learn how to lean on my current significant other to play the role of a mother figure in the home. Step-parents and foster parents have a lot in common. Step-parents don't have the luxury of knowing the history of the child, similarly to a foster parent. Together, these parents have to learn how to keep a harmonious vibe in the home – often on a very short-term basis.

Sound familiar? Foster parents have to do the same thing.

I learned a different kind of love

I had to love my kids no matter what. Going from living with my spouse and children to going through a divorce and moving away from my kids was excruciating. Going through that taught me how to love and care for my children in a different way. Going through that forced me to take inventory of what's important. Seeing my children on a part-time basis taught me the true definition of unconditional love. My limited time with them became especially important. However, I really do understand why there are "deadbeat dads" out there. It's not easy dealing with the ramifications of a hostile divorce. Carrying the burden of child support, the stresses of work, being a provider, and taking care of a home can be exhausting. Add to that, trying to move on and potentially develop new relationships can be an added layer of stress. Combine all of this with trying to maintain a shred of dignity. Juggling all of this is enough to make a strong man shrivel up and run away. I didn't say that I respected a man that would do that, but I can empathize and have since curbed my judgments.

The divisive nature of many divorces can intentionally or unintentionally sabotage relationships with kids. However, the same thing goes for a foster dad that has to deal with birth parents that are trying to get their kids back as well as the kids that desperately want to go home. Newsflash: many parents of the kids that we foster don't like us. Some birth parents don't appreciate the fact that we are only trying to love and care for their child while they get it together. Lots of times, parents of kids that come into our care view us as the enemy and will try everything in their power to disrupt any harmony that we are trying to create in our home. It's one of the most disturbing and disheartening things that a foster parent has to endure. Going through a divorce filled with scorn and spite made it easier for me to deal with a parent of any foster kid in my home. It was recognizable. I noticed it right away. I knew how to deal with it. The best tool in your toolbox is the unconditional love that you can offer a child. Love him or her without reservation or restriction just like you would your own. With a divorce, an ex can punch you in the stomach emotionally because of the history that the two of you share. A parent of a foster kid doesn't have that luxury. Simply put, they don't know you like that. There is no historical data that they can tap into in an attempt to rip your heart out. I'm not encouraging divorce here. I wouldn't wish that on anyone. However, I am encouraging foster parents that are trying to love on foster kids, to find a life experience that is relatable – one that you can use to parent your child with an unconditional care for their well-being.

The Bad

One week after Stephanie graduated from Grand Valley State University with a Bachelor's Degree in Social Work, she announced, "I've enrolled in the Masters of Social Work program at Western Michigan University."

I sighed, visibly frustrated.

"I knew that you'd be angry with me," she managed to squeak out.

"Hell yeah, I'm angry with you," I answered. "When were you going to talk to me about it?"

"This is exactly why I didn't talk to you about it because I knew how you'd respond," she barked back with her head cocked.

"Do you even have a clue as to why I am mad?" I asked quizzically.

"I don't know, probably because you want me to get a full-time job," she rebutted with a perturbed look.

"You damn skippy I want you to get a full-time job!" I yelled, completely angry now and standing over her as she sat at the dining room table.

"Don't be such an asshole! You know I am trying my best to raise my two kids while working a part-time job and going to school full-time. My dream is to get my Master's degree, and if I go to work full-time, I am afraid that I won't ever go back," she expressed while backing away from me and walking into the kitchen.

"I have been busting ass trying to make this mortgage payment while you go to school. And now you play the 'single mother' card? Newsflash, we are married! You're not a single mother; your two kids are my kids as Julia and Gunnor are yours. I bought this house for us but I could use some help here. When I got fired from my job from Pepsi, I didn't ask you to drop school to help because I knew that you were close to finishing. But now you're done, and you have more marketability. You can get a job and start a career. In doing so, we can catch the mortgage up. Not to mention, I want to see my kids!" I growl through clenched teeth, trying to control my anger and tone.

"It's not my fault that your ex-wife is a bitch and moved your kids to Arizona. It's not my fault that you signed a bad adjustable rate mortgage and you can't afford the payments because they went up.

It's not my fault that your child support is higher than the mortgage payment. Why should I have to put my plans on hold?" She screamed, six inches away from my face.

"Because we have to live in a house! We have to eat! I notice you keep saying your payments instead of our payments! I haven't seen my kids since Christmas! It's March! Could you go three months without seeing your kids? Could you live three thousand miles away from your kids and not know where they go to school? Who their friends are? If you had a full-time job, the extra income would at least free up some cash flow so I could go out for a visit. I miss my kids! I need to see them more, and all you can think about is how you *need* to go after *your* dreams. Well, I need to see my kids more! Which one do you think is more important?" I asked in an exasperated tone.

"You are always trying to make me feel guilty. God, you're selfish." She muttered weakly.

"I'm selfish? You're the most selfish woman I know. All I want to do is see my kids! You'll support that with words, but I need you to support that with actions." I screamed as I slammed the door and walked out.

Such was the theme of many of our arguments. Simply put, when Mandy moved my kids to Arizona, she took a piece of my heart with her. I wanted to move with them and I wanted Stephanie and her two kids to come with me. Being a dad from a distance was killing me. I felt as if I needed to do more. Julia was a freshman in high school. She needed her dad at that time more than ever. Gunnor was only eight years old, but his development was starting to be influenced by me. I was convinced that I needed to be there to mold him. The only way that I could see me being the best dad that I could be, and the best husband that I could be, was for all of us to move to Arizona. Even with Mandy only letting Julia and Gunnor see me sparingly, it was better than not being there at all.

Who was going to size up Julia's boyfriends? Who was going to teach Gunnor how to throw a tight spiral? I was extremely torn. How do I choose between my children and my marriage?

I finally made it out to Arizona for a visit and in doing so I surprised Gunnor at school. He was thrilled to see me and talked non-stop. On my second day there, on our way from school back to the hotel, Gunnor asked from the back seat of the car, "Dad, can't you just get a job here and move to Arizona?"

Tears started to swell. I tried to swallow the lump as I drove on the 101 Loop but the faucet just came on. I said, "Yes, Son. Yes I can."

Without another thought, I put the nearest ITT Tech into my GPS and followed it to Tempe. We jumped out of the car and went inside, asking to speak to the Director of Admissions. I introduced myself and gave her my credentials, which at the time were pretty impressive. I was the top Admissions Representative in Grand Rapids. After detailing my experience, I received a job offer right there at the Tempe location.

Three months later, I packed up everything that I could in my Ford Taurus and headed on the three-day journey west to the desert with one goal in mind; to be a better father for my kids. That journey was the start of the end of my marriage to Stephanie.

The problem with my decision was that I still had a wife and her two kids that I was responsible for. Stephanie was a couple classes away from finishing her Master's program. My goal, while not our goal, was for Stephanie and her two kids to join me in Phoenix. She never gave me a real guarantee that she would move, but that was my hope and plan anyway. In reality, Stephanie had no desire to leave Michigan, but would often pacify me by entertaining the notion. Her reasons were legitimate, I suppose; but, they would literally shut the conversation down. It put me on the defensive and caused us to argue and often led to fighting about something irrelevant.

She even went as far as convincing me that she was actively seeking employment in Arizona. But deep down, she knew she wasn't coming. I think on some level, I knew it too.

It wasn't all roses

No sooner than I got to Arizona, my ex-wife, Mandy wanted to go back to the parenting schedule that we had in Michigan. The original court order arrangement was five to eight p.m. on Wednesday and every other weekend. I moved three thousand miles away from home to be a better father and that was the route she wanted to go? Not to mention, my job wanted me to work two late nights a week and that would further cut into time that I could see my kids. I looked forward to anything school related because Mandy couldn't keep me away from track meets, basketball games, school concerts, or parent-teacher conferences.

During this tug-of-war parenting, my marriage to Stephanie was on very shaky ground. She was pulling away and the three thousand miles that separated us wasn't helping the situation, not to mention the toll that my absence was taking on Stephanie's two kids. I was also receiving calls from my dad and his doctors about his ailing health. I was losing control and spiraling into a mess!

My production at work started to slip. I stopped eating. I stopped exercising. I could feel myself falling into a depression and it didn't seem like I could do anything about it. I absolutely hated being alone and eating dinner alone was torture. On the positive side, I was making headway with my kids, or so I thought. But something was missing. I was still very incomplete.

I didn't feel whole. I missed my city, my home, and my wife. Simply put, I was homesick. It was time for me to make a decision... a big one! Ultimately, I knew I needed to go back home to Grand Rapids.

But how could I tell my kids that I was leaving them again? I sat down with my daughter Julia and had a very adult conversation.

"What's the matter, Dad? You don't seem yourself," she asked in a concerned tone.

Slowly, I replied, "Jules, you're right. I'm not."

Julia, still looking concerned, asked, "You want to talk about it?"

"Yeah, your Papa isn't doing too well," I said, fighting back tears at the mention of my Dad.

She sighed and pressed further, "What's wrong with him?"

"Parkinson's. You know how he shakes? The shakes are winning and it's causing dementia," I uttered.

"What else?" She asked.

"Isn't that enough?" I said, confused.

"Well you seem unhappy. You're not smiling. It's like you're here but you're not. It's like you're somewhere else." She said, intuitively.

"It's grown-up stuff," I managed to say weakly, trying to avoid the fact that the answer wasn't good enough.

"I miss Stephanie." I finally uttered under my breath.

"And Deuce and Trina?" She said, correctly knowing who I really missed.

"Yes, and Deuce and Trina," I replied.

After a pause, Julia takes the defensive. "I thought she was coming here? Is she?" She asked angrily.

"No, I don't think that she is coming here. You'll have to ask her," I replied, knowing she wasn't.

"What's the biggest reason you want to go home?" asked Julia.

I responded by stating, "I need to save my marriage. But it's hard because I don't want to leave you and your brother."

"Dad, I am old enough for me to tell you this so don't take this the wrong way. It is ok for you to go back to Grand Rapids. Gunz and I will be fine. Mom takes good care of us. Yeah, it's been fun having you here. But Deuce and Trina need you more than we do. I don't really understand why Stephanie doesn't want to come here, but I'm sure it has to do with her not wanting to leave her family and taking the kids out of their school. I didn't want to leave my school when I moved here, so I'm sure Trina doesn't want to leave hers," my wise daughter told me.

"Would you be disappointed if I left and went home back to Michigan?" I asked nervously.

Her eyes began to brim with tears but she continued for my sake. "I'd be selfish if I kept you all to myself. You've raised me to make tough decisions and live with them...good or bad. Besides, we have more fun and spend more time with you when we come home for holidays and breaks. If you stay here, that would go away and I don't think that we would see Deuce and Trina nearly as much as we do now."

Without another thought, I embraced her and repeated how much I loved her.

Through my shirt, she muttered "I know you do or else you wouldn't be here. I love you too."

"To da moon?" I said playfully

"And back," she said, through her pretty smile.

I was floored. I thought to myself, "This little girl is amazing – wise beyond her years."

She could've said, "I don't want you to leave," and I would've stayed right there in Phoenix without a question! What that taught me is to never underestimate a child; never discount what they are thinking or assume that they are not of age. It's okay to have a tough conversation with children because they can take it. Not only can they take it, but they need to have those conversations. If you "sugarcoat" anything with a kid in foster care they will see right through it. You have to be transparent. If you're not, they will eat you alive and spit out the parts that they don't like. They will hold it against you for not being real with them. Having gone through this with my own child, I am now able to have a hard, and necessary conversation with a teenage kid as it relates to their current situations.

Foster kids will ask me questions about their current situation. I have no problem telling them exactly what is going to happen, or as much as I know, and how I see things playing out. All the while, I am constantly reassuring them that I'm there for them. I convince them that I will love them regardless of the outcome. They know that I will support them always. Once you have had those difficult conversations with a kid in foster care, you begin to earn trust. It then becomes easier for them to ask you questions. They will start to confide in you because of the rapport and the foundation that you have laid. If you tap dance around difficult subjects and give them a superficial answer then they will see right through you. Good luck trying to get that trust back!

The Ugly

If my divorce from Mandy was hard, then my divorce from Stephanie was torture!

Stephanie and I had some work to do, a marriage to repair, but I was determined to make things work. I had a new-found mission. I didn't want to have a second failed marriage and I also didn't want to let Julia down. If I was going to leave her and her brother to save my marriage then that was what I intended to do. I jumped through all the hoops - therapy, counseling, self-discovery, transformation, cutting off friends, etc. If she asked for it, I did it, but it didn't work. The damage had been done. I sensed that there was trouble in the air. I smelled the deceptive vibe that Stephanie was putting out. Karma had come to tap dance on my emotions and make a playground out of my soul. My 'Spidey' senses were tingling and, because of them, I made the ultimate sign of insecurity move.

After a so-called "night out" on a Tuesday, Stephanie came home after two in the morning and she didn't smell like the bar, instead her hair smelled like strawberry essence shampoo. This was weird. So what did I do? I checked her purse. I was looking for anything, anything that would tell me where she had been or what she had done. What I found was much worse. I found a receipt from Walgreens and her purchase included shampoo, razors, deodorant, pantyhose, and condoms. I could feel my heart drop into the middle of my stomach and I literally could not breathe. I started the pizza breathing technique that the therapist taught me back in Arizona.

After regaining the air in my lungs, I went into the kitchen to look inside the Walgreens bag and crosscheck; maybe there was an explanation. I saw all of the items mentioned but the condoms.

Whoa?

I stormed into the room, clicked on the light, and screamed, "Stephanie, wake up! Who are you $##$ing? If you lie to my face, I am going to start slugging." It only escalated from there. I kept screaming, pounding walls, and slamming doors, all because of this overwhelming desire to pound her face and to slam her body into the wall. Suddenly, I remembered what my dad told me, "Son, if you ever feel the need to hit a woman, then you should just walk away." Remembering that forced me to wake up and remember there were sleeping kids in the house.

I simply left and drove to my good friend Margaret's house, trying to smell the pizza the whole way there. I couldn't believe how calm I was while talking to Margaret. She was such a good friend; she didn't give me any advice, she just listened and helped me process. It was four o'clock in the morning and I was sitting in her living room baring my soul.

In the morning, I called Stephanie and she answered on the first ring. I told her that I forgave her for what she had done.

How could I not forgive her for something that I had done to her?

How could I not forgive her after all that I had put her through?

When I got home I was still hurt but more dazed and confused like a tired, punch-drunk boxer in the ninth round of a title fight. I told her that we would talk about it tomorrow. I went to work and stumbled through the day. I was like a zombie, but my friend Margaret was there to hold me up and make sure I didn't snap.

After work, I immediately wanted to talk about everything. The anger and the rage came right back when she wouldn't tell me who she was "creeping" with. I was crushed and devastated but I was still determined to make it work; even more so now than ever.

A couple of months went by and we were still doing the counseling thing and trying to repair the damage, but my insecurities were still on edge. I had a heightened alert to my day-to-day that made me paranoid. It was as if karma was slapping me around and daring me to say something. I even went so far as trying to check her phone records. When I tried, I was told that she had put a passcode lock on our T-mobile account. I made the decision to break the code.

Number sequence number one denied...

Number two denied...

DEUTINA (combination of her two kids names)...Jackpot, I was in.

Once I had cracked it, I realized it was the worst thing I could've done. Checking the phone records told me everything I needed to know. It was like I had a pair of prescription glasses that gave me instant clarity into the past. It brought into focus everything that didn't add up for months... even years. She had started cheating when I left for Phoenix. It even started months before I left.

I was devastated, demoralized, defeated, and done!

Unfortunately, her two kids Deuce and Trina had front row seats to our demise. Regrettably, they heard more than they should have. At one point during a heated argument, I heard Trina screaming at both of us, "You guys should trust and love each other! Stop fighting." She was only twelve and Deuce was fifteen.

Our marriage was damaged beyond repair. Upon our divorce, I knew that the relationship with my step-children was over as I knew it. Some pretty hurtful things had been said and it wasn't like I was going to tell them my side of a very bad story. Indirectly, Deuce and Trina received a one-sided, very jaded story of our split by their mom and her friends. Her friends verbally told them how I was such an ass for the way that I treated their mom, which showed that they clearly didn't know the whole story.

In the divorce discussions, Stephanie said she wanted me to pay some of her student loans back and that was something that I was willing to fight about.

"Yeah right! Am I going to receive half of your future wages too? Get the fuck out of here!" I screamed sarcastically.

I told her she could take me to court if she wanted to because I had learned from the debacle with Mandy. I was fully prepared to crush her in open court. Ultimately, Stephanie didn't want any part of that. A referee that seemed to be on my side from the start of the proceedings, ruled in my favor which fueled the fire even more. She pursued the dream of completing a Master's Degree so as far as I was concerned, she could endure the nightmare of over ninety thousand dollars' worth of student loans. She hated me and told me to not even think about contacting her kids.

For the second time, in my adult life, I was leaving my home with the clothes on my back. I was starting over once again. I had been here before; however, this time I was a grown man with experience instead of a scared teenager.

Trauma all over again.

The next year was rough for me, to say the least; I was an emotional train-wreck. Over a six-month stretch, I had experienced the following traumatic experiences according to my therapist.

- I left my kids in Arizona
- I left my job to be with my wife Stephanie
- I discovered my wife Stephanie having an affair
- I left the home that I paid for with the clothes on my back
- My dad died
- I was served divorce papers

I had loved Stephanie. I put my heart out there and made myself more vulnerable than ever before with her.

So, how did I get through our divorce? I'm still getting through it. I moved in with my good friend and co-worker Margaret, went to therapy weekly for almost a year, and wrote. I continue to write even today. I felt as if I was writing for my life and, for the second time, writing became my best coping skill. The pen became my best friend.

What does this have to do with foster care? Everything! Being forced away from Stephanie was hard; walking away from Deuce and Trina was worse, but I had to save myself. I was fighting a woman who hated me, for parenting time, to kids that weren't biologically mine. I battled kids that felt betrayed and abandoned by me – all while having their heads filled with a one-sided story about my character. It was too much for me to withstand. I had to save myself and let them go. I sat them both down and told them that I loved them and that I'd always be there for them. I told them how sorry I was for the way things played out. But, I would have to love them from a distance. Despite our relationship being on the fence, I hugged them and repeated how much I loved them. Over the next few months, I tried to keep in touch with them but the constant rejection took its toll. I gave them my contact information and told them that I was just a phone call away. If they ever needed me, they could call day or night.

Divorcing Stephanie would ultimately help prepare me to be a foster dad. I learned how to let a kid go home to his mom and love them from a distance. The same approach that I took with my step-children, is the same measure I take with a kid in foster care that I have to send home.

Sending a child home that you have grown attached to is extremely hard. However, it's different because when choosing to provide foster care, you go into it knowing that it's intended to be a temporary situation. It takes the sting out a little bit when you know that the ultimate goal is reunification with their biological parents. Instead of mourning the loss, I celebrate the win of a child going home to his family. Foster parents are a necessary step in that child's journey. Most children will love their parents blindly while forgiving anything that has been done to them directly or indirectly. Take my dad for example. After all of the wrong he did, I still would've given anything to go home if he were there. I take comfort in knowing that it is not the child's fault and ultimately I am doing the absolute best that I can to offer a sense of stability and love – even if only for a short time.

Thoughts of a Foster Dad: Key Beliefs and Takeaways

- Assume that the children that you are taking into your home have seen and heard it all. Most times they have. When kids come into a foster care situation, nine times out of ten they have seen and been a part of the worst possible situations.

- Foster care placements are designed to be temporary. However, you will have a permanent impact on their lives. It is a responsibility not to be taken lightly. You have to love that child and treat that child as if he/she will be with you forever. If you don't, then you don't go in all the way emotionally when the kid needs you to. It is also imperative that no promises of "forever" are made until there is certainty that the child can become part of your forever family.

- Take your own personal baggage with relationships and use those experiences to your advantage. If you have been through something hurtful, use your experience to teach the foster kid in your home the best way to get through their own hurts. They are suffering from a loss that is consuming their everyday ability to think clearly. They need your help to get through it.

- When you send a child back to their parents then it is time for a celebration. Do just that. Celebrate! Mission accomplished! The ultimate goal is a successful reunification. If your paths happen to cross again, then be prepared to be there for that child in whatever way possible, within reason.

- Be transparent. Don't be afraid to open up to a foster child about your past experiences, good and bad. It's a part of the getting to know each other process. How can it be expected for them to share everything with you and you not be willing to share everything with them? In doing so, it humanizes you. You then can help to chisel away that protective emotional armor that they have. It will help to create some trust between the two of you. I openly tell my foster children about my past triumphs and failures in an effort to teach them lessons learned from my mistakes.

Chapter 8: Random Thoughts

During the process of writing this book, I kept a page open so that I could collect random ideas and thoughts related to my journey, relationships and the children I've raised. These thoughts quickly formed into a chapter of their own. I have found this to be one of the most therapeutic things that I have ever done.

"I wonder what he's thinking."

"Who does he look like?"

"Has he ever met his dad?"

"Still bed-wetting. Why?"

"Did he fight a lot when he was in residential?"

"He's been abused."

"He's been neglected."

"I wonder if he was ever molested."

"1 + 1 does not equal 2 for him."

"He has no logic…if he does then, I don't understand it."

"He has an inability to reason."

"His perception is reality."

"His self-esteem is really low."

"I just want him to succeed."

"Why doesn't he want it as bad as I do?"

"I just want to help him."

"I can't do the work for him, I can only show him."

"I can't parent every child the same."

"I often think that I don't know what the hell I'm doing."

"You are raising what you think is a successful biological son…the same formula can't be used with your foster son."

"Why does he lie so much?"

"He lied to me seven times already today and its only 1 p.m."

"He hasn't left the basement in three days, I wonder if he's depressed."

"He called me dad today…I smiled on the inside."

"He called me Julian today. What happened to dad? Probably because he was mad at me."

"I hate the way they disrespect my wife."

"The way he talks to me and the way he talks to my wife is different. It's as if he doesn't respect her and knows that he will get his way."

"Every woman that has ever come into his life has failed him."

"No wonder he hates female figures."

"I want to discipline them the same way that I would Gunnor. With Gunnor, I can yell at him to redirect him. Yelling at the other boys the same way will trigger them into a scared fight, flight, freeze, state of mind."

"I saw fear in his eyes when I yelled at him."

"His last foster dad yelled at him before he beat him."

"I have to pay attention to how I speak to him and take a different approach."

"I know that I can't spank him, but sometimes I want to."

"I feel inadequate and sometimes unequipped to parent him."

"His attitude towards me angers me and scares me at the same time."

"He could use a good ass-whooping right now."

"He is so afraid when I yell at him. I can see the fear in his eyes and his body language."

"He shuts down."

"I must remember that they were once abused."

"My triggers as a kid caused me to lash out at him today."

"If only he knew how much I love him."

"I wonder if he knows."

"His friends really like us."

"I can tell that he didn't take his meds today."

"It took him a whole year to have a sleepover at a friend's house."

"I'm happy he is able to form healthy attachments and have friends."

"Why won't she take a shower?"

"He tries to sabotage every friendship he has."

"He has friends that don't have dads in their lives."

"They all spend a lot of time at our house."

"I wonder if they see me as a father figure and gravitate towards me."

"Some of his friends are truly one phone call away from foster care themselves."

"I hate being a mandated reporter."

"Holidays must be hard for them."

"I wonder what he thinks when he looks in the mirror."

"Does he wonder who he looks like?"

"It's gotta suck to not have any baby pictures."

"My wife is my rock."

"She is an awesome mom."

"I sometimes wish that she can experience child-birth."

"We would make great-looking kids."

"Gunnor looks a lot like we made him together."

"I hope that is enough for her."

"I'm afraid that she will resent me for not giving her a biological child."

"Her parents would love a biological grandchild."

"I often think about reversing my vasectomy procedure in an attempt to make everyone happy."

"I sometimes regret having the vasectomy procedure."

"I have to tell Julia that we will become foster parents."

"It is important to me that Julia is supportive of our decision to become foster parents."

"I hope she is excited."

"Gunnor will have some more brothers and sisters."

"I hope he doesn't think that I am trying to replace him."

"Today we took in a new placement, I hope that he sleeps well."

"I think he is bi-racial."

"I think he is relieved that he looks like me."

"I think he is happy that we look the part of his parents."

"With him being light skinned it helps the public perception. It will also make it a little easier for him to call us his parents verbally without anyone batting an eye."

"My dark-skinned sons don't have this luxury."

"I wonder if it bothers them."

"Stares from random people when were out is hard on everyone."

"Black kids, white mom, people stare a lot."

"He is a really big kid, I wonder how big he'll get."

"Wow he can really eat for only being fifteen years old."

"He wants to call me dad but he is hesitant."

"Stacey is finally happy that a kid actually wants to spend time with her."

"He really likes Stacey and seems to be attached to her hip."

"He wants to be adopted by us."

"Little does he know that he has to adopt us too."

"Is this kid really this good or is he still honeymooning?"

"I wonder what he looked like as a baby."

"My niece is having a baby and she is excited and so is the whole family."

"She is having a baby shower."

"I wish we could have a baby shower for a fifteen year old."

"Why isn't our family as happy for us that we have a fifteen year old?"

"Fifteen year olds are kids too."

"I want my family to be as supportive as if we were giving birth."

"The day we adopted Michael and Andre, there was a celebration."

"We should celebrate it like it is a birthday party."

"It was on the same day as Stacey's birthday."

"She was really happy."

"Sometimes I want to be evaluated."

"I want to know that we are making progress."

"The placement worker called and asked if we'd take another placement."

"They are willing to make exceptions to the already full house that we have."

"Are we that good or is our agency that desperate for families?"

"Black teenage boys are hard to place."

"I wonder if it is because of the lack of black families willing to do foster care."

"Most people that foster are white."

"They often times prefer babies."

"Everyone wants babies."

"I wonder what they truly see or think when they see a teenage black boy?"

"Is he a threat?"

"Do they feel threatened by him?"

"Do they think he is too damaged?"

"Will they be judged by their friends?"

"Will we be judged by our friends?"

"I wonder if the stereotype is true."

"He really wants to see his bio mom but can't because the courts said that she was unsafe."

"How do I decipher the difference between foster care problems and normal teenage problems?"

"He is a master manipulator."

"He has been with us for three years and is still hoarding food under his bed."

"She just purposely pissed off the whole family."

"She is pregnant."

"I don't think that she can handle another man that she loves being disappointed in her."

"I will trigger her if I yell."

"She has officially shut me out. It makes me feel like a failure."

"She is really pretty but her self-esteem is terribly low."

"Do teenage black boys get categorized by society as at-risk, making it harder for them to be fostered?"

"I wish I could save them all."

"One day Dre's friend came over and never left."

"He calls me dad now."

"One of the boys on my basketball team is a friend with one of my sons. He randomly asked if he could live with us. I laughingly said no. With tears in his eyes, he expressed he was serious."

"Boundaries...I have to learn how to practice them as much as the kids do."

"I am lacking compassion today. I don't like this feeling."

DID I REALLY HEAR THAT?

"I need his real mom to sign for that."

"You can't be his mom."

"Are those your real kids?"

"What's his story?"

"Why can't you have kids of your own? If people only knew how very painful and personal this question is."

"Is that your boyfriend? Stacey gets that question a lot."

"How do you feed them all?"

"Damn, you have a lot of kids. You must get food stamps."

"Why do you care for all of those kids if they aren't yours?"

"Why don't they look like you?"

"Shouldn't he be better by now?"

"When is he going to be normal?"

"Do you get paid to take care of all of those kids?"

"Black people only do it for the money."

"The only reason I won't foster is because I can't whoop them."

Chapter 9: Finding Your Niche

Welcome to the five percent club!

Only five percent of teenagers in the foster care system, age fifteen or older, are adopted by a family.

After adopting our two boys — Dre, fifteen, and Michael, seventeen — my wife and I have now become a part of the five percent.

"Julian, I need you to come into the office today. Bring your laptop with you for review." The text message read that popped up on my company Blackberry from Ralph, the Sales & Merchandising Manager at Country Fresh. Country Fresh is a dairy company that supplied the entire state of Michigan and a majority of the Midwest. I pulled up to the office in the company-leased car, hopped out to grab my laptop, and jetted upstairs to the second floor. The corporate offices are on top of the dairy plant. When I walked in, the first person I saw was Dawn, our administrative assistant and someone I truly admire for all the sales support she offered me in my role as an Account Manager. After some pleasantries about the MSU Spartans pounding the Hoosiers the night before, I asked her where Ralph is. She pointed me to the Human Resources Office and I skeptically headed into the room. Inside were Ralph and some Human Resources lady that I had never met before. After we exchanged hellos, I had a seat.

Without a pause, Ralph began by saying, "Julian we have to let you go."

"Huh?" I asked, reeling from what felt like getting kicked in the nuts. I looked around the crowded and unorganized office with no windows and paperwork spread out everywhere.

Ralph simply gave me a blank stare.

"For what?" I asked hastily. "Does this have anything to do with Meijer buying Bareman Dairy?" Meijer was our number one customer and Bareman was our number one competitor. Earlier that month I saw on the news that Meijer had actually bought Bareman Dairy and had plans to complete millions of dollars in renovations.

Without an answer, I continued but am getting more and more upset by a lack of answers. "Ralph?! Is this happening to anyone else on our sales team? Or is it me?"

Ralph simply gives me a blank stare.

I could tell he would have rather been anywhere else but there right at that moment. He respected me, as he had just given me a sales award and a bonus for hitting my numbers a few weeks earlier.

"Ralph?" I pushed. I just wanted something. Anything.

"Julian, I am not allowed to tell you what may happen to others. Right now it's just you. You had a couple of unsatisfactory reviews on your last two evaluations."

"Then how did I receive a bonus?" I inquired. None of this made sense.

Ralph, getting red in the face, cut off the conversation, saying, "Julian, I need your laptop, your phone, your security keycard, and the keys to the car. I will escort you to your vehicle so that you can remove any personal belongings you have. I'm sorry it has come to this. I wish you good luck in your future endeavors."

I stood up and shook his hand and walked out, amazingly keeping my composure together. I was determined to keep my dignity and walked out with my head held high. After I boxed up my belongings, Ralph drove me home; it was the most awkward car ride ever. We both knew what was happening was crap, but I was still filled with this overwhelming desire to sock him right in his face! I called my wife Stacey and told her that I had been fired and, after asking me if I was okay, she talked to me on the phone the whole way home.

Once I got home, Stacey embraced me with a long hug.

"We saw this coming you know. You know what you're worth. You're awesome. I'd hire you," she attempted to console me.

"Thanks, Babe. But this hurts." I answered, with a wounded tone. At this point, we were in the car headed to D. A. Blodgett-St. Johns, the foster care agency that held our foster care license.

"Seriously! We are supposed to sign all this paperwork today so that Michael and Andre can come and live with us. How am I supposed to take care of my family if I don't have a job?"

"God will find a way," Stacey said convincingly.

"Well right now God has a funny way of showing it," I replied.

"We will be ok," she said in a soothing tone.

"I always land on my feet and this is just another hurdle. But today? Why today? Why do I get fired from my job on the same day that we are taking our two new boys home? Is it a sign that maybe we shouldn't be doing this right now?" I asked weakly.

Somewhat hurt by my response, Stacey responded, "Lovie, once we decided to take this step they are forever ours. Just because one of us loses our jobs doesn't mean that we do anything different when it comes to our kids. Everything will be fine."

We pull up to the foster care agency and walked into one of the conference rooms where there were about six people, all middle-aged white ladies with various social worker titles and credentials. My wife was also a social worker in the child welfare arena. So while she wasn't their co-worker (she worked for a different agency), she was amongst her peers. She knew the lingo, spoke the language, and she had led many meetings like this. This one; however, was a little different because, this time, she was on the opposite end of the table. This time, the meeting was about her, her boys and her new and growing family. It was personal.

This meeting was the start of #TeamGoodson. As I looked across the table, I was extremely grateful for Stacey's skills, experience, and know-how. I was still in a daze from everything that had transpired earlier. I was there but things were fuzzy. She was my eyes when I couldn't see and my ears when I couldn't hear.

This group meeting was a transition plan for the boys, and quite honestly, I wondered if the kids living with them hoped to be rescued in some way. Institutional residential homes are not meant to be a permanent or a long-term solution, but often times it seems like the young people are there forever.

Over the next few weeks, the boys came to our house for visits every day. The last Friday of the month was the big day. That was the day the boys would move to their new home. Our home. We went to the group home and helped our boys gather up all of their belongings. Helping them to decide what to keep and what to take was difficult. To me, some of their items looked like they needed to be thrown away. But to them, they were their most prized possessions. They didn't want to throw anything away and, at first, I just chalked it up to them being pack-rats. Watching them grab everything they owned and pack a garbage bag bothered me though. That's when it hit me. Their possessions were all they had and I had just been encouraging them to throw it all away. I felt terrible and I remember saying to myself that their stuff wasn't garbage.

I also thought, "The next time I do this, I am going to bring a brand new suitcase so that the child can move with dignity."

I was excitedly nervous. Not only because they were coming into my home but because I had no idea what my next career move would be, just as I was adding two new mouths to feed.

A blessing in disguise

As it turned out, getting fired from my job helped our new family a lot. I had time on my hands. We had a small cushion of savings. I received some severance and unemployment money to help us out. And to mention, Stacey's aunt let me borrow a car to drive until I could figure things out. At that point, I knew we would be set for a couple of months. Besides, it was the end of the summer and football practices were just starting.

Our school district, Wyoming Public, had two high schools, Wyoming Park and Wyoming Rogers. But because of budget cutting, the two schools were combining. It was perfect timing for Michael and Andre since all the students would be going to a new school. The extra time I had was useful for getting the boys acclimated to a new community, a new school, and a new environment. After enrolling them in school, we went and introduced ourselves to the football coaches, the most important people they wanted to meet. After discussing them playing on the team, it was set. The boys would start practicing right away.

During my time off, I did all of the things that I would have relied on my wife to do. If I were working, I wouldn't have been able to establish a relationship with the boys as fast as I did. A huge part of our relationship building was our mutual love for football. They were seeking my validation and I had the time to give it to them by being at everything that required extra attention. I dropped them off and picked them up every day from practice. That simple practice built trust. If they trusted me then they were more likely to feel safe. The walls came down slowly. They'd get in the car and I'd ask them how practice was, then shut up and listen. I needed them to have a sense of purpose. Football gave them that. A foundation of consistency was being laid. I went from bread-winner to caregiver in a matter of months.

After a few months of constant connecting and bonding, it was time for me to do something else. I was restless. I had been working since I was fourteen years old, and without a job, I was bored out of my mind. Being a stay-at-home dad was cool for a little while, but I had to start moving. It was important for me to show my teenage boys that men work, men provide, men take care of the family no matter what. I would not let them see me, a black man, staying home while my wife, a white woman, went to work every day. There was no way that I was feeding into that stereotype. I couldn't tell them to do certain things that I wasn't doing myself. It was time to show them and get back into the race.

After flopping around for months, doing odd jobs and taking jobs that didn't fit me, I finally hit "pay dirt." I took a Business Account Management position with Sprint. I thought that with twenty years of sales experience, it was only a matter of time before I found something meaningful: good salary, benefits, upside growth potential, the whole nine yards. After working there for approximately one month, though, I'd had enough. After a heart to heart with my wife one night, the next morning I walked into my sales manager's office and resigned. I discovered that I was completely burned out with sales.

I couldn't stomach the fact that I was doing something I absolutely despised. It was time for me to pursue something that I loved. My boys had to see me going after my dreams and goals with both hands while being happy in the process. Teenagers in foster care who have been in the system for years are incredibly observant and can spot a fraud from a mile away. It didn't matter how much money I made or what I was able to say I had because that didn't matter to them. What did matter, however, was the impression of how I came home after a long day's work, and ultimately, it was more important for me to be there for them emotionally. I needed to be there, to be present and alert.

Dinner time had become the most important time of the day, especially for our kids who needed structure and routine. The time spent at the dinner table became an instant comedy routine. It provided a sense of normalcy that everyone in our family needed.

I stepped out on faith

After countless conversations with my wife about "what I wanted to be when I grow up." I finally started to move my feet. I was also reading a book by a good friend of mine Kris Mathis, "*From Success to Significance.*" It was inspiring. I always felt that I wanted to be a teacher and a coach because I loved coaching basketball, and I really loved being in the gym. But going back to school to pursue a teaching degree was something that I didn't have the luxury of pursuing, nor did I want to, so I started to volunteer my time. I began to mentor young men which was easy to do since my sons always had friends around. Little did I know that mentoring my kids' friends would be the start of something extremely significant.

Once I gained that experience, I started a part-time, temporary position as a Youth Development Specialist with the Grand Rapids Urban League and worked with the young "Urban Fellows." The Urban Fellows is a summer job program. I was responsible for about twenty young men between the ages of thirteen and seventeen. We specialized in college and career preparation, community outreach, volunteering, mentoring, and neighborhood clean-up. Little did those boys know, but they were helping me just as much as I was helping them. I couldn't teach them the importance of following their passion and making a career out of it if I wasn't doing it myself. So every activity they did or that I taught them, I used as an opportunity to sharpen my skills. With the help of my Grand Rapids Urban League co-worker, I taught resume building workshops, mock interviewing skills, and the importance of vision boards. Doing all of that would help me not only with my career, but with my boys as well.

Right around the same time, I also started to volunteer my time with a girls AAU basketball club called the West Michigan Drive, directed by a good friend of mine. I had a team of fourteen to fifteen-year-old girls from all over West Michigan. I began to build a foundation of trust and guidance with not only the girls but their families as well. My goal was to teach them life lessons through the game of basketball.

Because I stepped out on faith, my dreams were coming true. I was in a conference room in front of a whiteboard with twenty youth looking up at me, hanging on every word I spoke. I was teaching! I was in the huddle with ten girls looking up at me, with a board, a dry erase marker in hand, drawing up a play with seconds left in the finals of the State AAU tournament. I was coaching! I always thought that I had to be in a school district to pursue this dream.

God had other plans all along, but it took me moving my feet to recognize the signs. I was genuinely passionate about doing both jobs and people took notice. My efforts later landed me a Youth Development position with Bethany Christian Services. Not to mention, the parents of my basketball team enjoyed the development and direction I instilled in their daughters so much, that they got together and paid me a small salary. I was moving my feet. I had no idea how it would work out but it did. For the first time in my career, I took money off the table when accepting a position and, for the first time in my career, I felt and knew that I was doing the right thing. Sales was always something that I was good at, but teaching and coaching was something that I loved and would do for free. I was using the talents that God instilled in me to teach the youth what I knew.

Stacey and I quickly became "that couple." We were the parents that teenagers gravitated to. Going to a high school basketball game on a Friday night became our definition of a date night. We both enjoy being around teenagers, we both coached girls basketball programs allowing us a necessary balance between the many young men we had at home. We do very well with teenagers-especially with African-American boys. We feel as though, we have so much to offer them.

As with anything, ideally things should be as close to the right fit as possible; foster care is no different. When finding a niche within a family structure and looking to take a placement, it's important to be realistic about your existing limitations and abilities. I am passionate about helping teenage boys become successful young men, so naturally my niche is working with young black youth. Why? I was once a struggling black teenager who became a man. I know what they are going through and I feel that I am a good person to teach them how to find success since I was once walked in their shoes.

Thoughts of a Foster Dad: Key Beliefs and Takeaways

- Commit. Once you commit to a foster kid, there is no turning back. Many adults have failed them up until this point. The fact that I lost my job changed nothing about the fact that Michael and Andre still needed and deserved a loving home.
- Balance – cultivating a parent-child relationship with a foster kid takes time. If you are constantly at work and on the go, chasing the corporate dream, you may be missing out on what's important.
- A good partner. Your partner has to compliment you in the areas that you are weak. Foster care has to be a team decision and not just one-sided. If one spouse has to talk the other spouse into foster care and adoption, then it is a bad idea.
- Everyone has something to offer a child in need. EVERYONE! Find what you do well and apply it. If your efforts are genuine, then the kid will naturally be excited about the energy you bring to the relationship.
- Men can be and should be nurturing and in touch with the emotional scars that a foster kid will bring to the table. Men can be stay-at-home-dads and can be well respected for it. Believe me, if you're doing it right, it can be a full-time job.

Chapter 10:

Alphabet Soup

> *Looking at all of my son's different diagnosis was as if someone took all of the letters of the alphabet and shook them up. It looked like a bowl of alphabet soup.*

> *30% of former foster care children are diagnosed with PTSD, which is about twice the rate of U.S. combat veterans.*

"Your son has ODD," said our son's counselor.

"What is ODD?" I asked, confused.

"Oppositional Defiance Disorder," he responded, seeming very self-assured

Still confused, I stuttered, "Ummm? What? What does that mean?"

"It means exactly what it says," the counselor responded without even blinking an eye.

"You're joking right?" I said. "Don't all kids have ODD?" I was chuckling now, trying to break the awkward tension that was settling in the room.

The counselor responded in even fashion, "I promise you, Mr. Goodson. It's real. Your son has never been in a position to make decisions for himself. That said, he will fight for every opportunity to do so. Authority figures especially, will feel his wrath."

I skeptically stare, thinking, "Okay, we'll see about that."

The counselor asked, "Have you noticed that he is very hard to redirect?"

"That's an understatement. I've never seen anything like it." I smugly responded.

"ODD is the reason," said the counselor.

"Your son has also been diagnosed with RAD, which stands for Reactive Attachment Disorder." The counselor said with more concern.

"HUH?" I replied, increasingly confused.

"It's uncommon but serious. He was unable to form a healthy bond with his primary parents. As a baby, he cried when he was hungry, and no one fed him. As a baby, he cried when his diaper was wet, and no one changed him. From what we know, when he cried, his three year old brother held him. In other words, he was severely neglected." The counselor explained in detail.

Tears welled up in my eyes, "that's awful," I replied.

"RAD develops when a child's most basic needs for nurturing, affection, and comfort have not been met. This stops them from forming healthy relationships with others. Your child will struggle with the basics of maintaining friends. It may likely take years for him to attach to you and your wife. He will intentionally and unintentionally sabotage relationships," the counselor explained.

"Wow!" Overwhelmed with emotions, I excused myself and left the room again.

I returned from the bathroom, "I'm sorry...I needed a minute. This is all so overwhelming and very emotional," I muttered.

"Mr. Goodson I know that this is a lot to take in. It can be very overwhelming. Are you ready to continue?" Asked the counselor.

I responded "Yeah," sniffling and wiping my nose, as I regained my composure.

The counselor pressed on, "There is more. Your son is also diagnosed with ADHD."

"Really?!" I responded with some excitement. "See...I have a serious issue with this one. How can a kid that has ADHD play video games for two straight hours? He doesn't move for hours sometimes. He can't possibly have ADHD."

"Your son will have a constant struggle with impulsiveness and inattention. His hyperactivity mixed with the others, will interfere with his academic, occupational or social performance," the counselor rebutted in a dry but concerned tone.

I replied, trying to sound somewhat educated on the subject, "I understand the concept, but he is performing well in school right now. He has been performing well since he came to live with us. Our goal is to give him some structure, guidance, and a lot of love. He was failing almost every class when he first came to us. Currently, he is boasting a 3.0 grade point average. He's never been that strong academically before, or so we've been told."

Setting me straight, the counselor replied, "His medication mixed with structure will help tremendously with his progress. He has a routine right now, which is great. Right now his schedule is waking up at six-thirty in the morning, taking his medicine, and going to school, football practice, home, homework, and then dinner. The Vyvanse he is taking will help him stay focused. The structure will give him something to look forward to. Keep up the good work."

"Is there anything else that he has been diagnosed with?" I asked, but nervous of the answer I'd receive.

"Yes, there is. PTSD," the counselor said with bass in his voice.

"Huh? Really?" I confusingly replied, "He is only thirteen years old. He has never been to war."

"Yes. Your son has Post-Traumatic Stress Disorder. It is a mental health disorder, which looks like battle fatigue occurring after a "traumatic" event that is outside the range of usual human experience. It is characterized by symptoms such as reliving the event, reduced involvement with others, and manifestations of autonomic arousal such as hyper alertness and exaggerated startle response," replied the counselor.

I sat there with my mouth open in amazement.

The counselor continued, "It is not uncommon for a child who has experienced the things he has, to experience effects on his mental health."

"Our son has the same symptoms as a war veteran?" I asked in a quizzical tone.

"Yes! In his mind, he has been to war. All of the trauma that he has faced in his young life has caused some behaviors that are very similar to a war veteran that has experienced trauma during battle. Those moments when you are unable to define his behaviors, are his brain reliving the event. If you yell at him, it may trigger a traumatic event that happened when he was beaten as a child. He will relive that experience all over again," explained the counselor.

I sat there with a dumbfounded look, jaw dropped, and an emotional lump formed in my throat... I felt guilty for ever yelling at him. "Is there anything else?" I managed to ask.

"No those are all of his diagnoses. ADHD, RAD, ODD, PTSD. All that remains is to review his IEP."

IEP? "I thought you were done with his diagnosis?" I replied laughingly, a weak attempt at humor. We both chuckled.

Still laughing, the counselor responded, "No, he has an Individualized Education Plan."

"Oh, I know what that is, but go on," I told him.

The counselor explained, "Your son's IEP is a legally binding document that spells out exactly what special education services he will receive and why. His plan includes classification, placement, services such as a one-on-one aide and therapies. It will also include academic goals, behavioral goals, and a behavioral plan. If needed, a percentage of time in regular education, and progress reports from teachers and therapists will be provided. The IEP is planned at an IEP meeting. The IEP meeting will have professionals such as: School Principal, School Social Worker, School Psychologist, Behavioral Specialist, Core Teachers, and a Special Education Teacher."

The counselor explains further, "He is a smart kid but has a hard time concentrating. Reading will be hard for him. He is allowed extra time to complete his work, and normally does well if the teacher reads the test to him."

"I have a lot to read up on. Thank you for explaining all of this to me. It is a bit overwhelming, but this meeting was extremely helpful for me." I said to him, standing and shaking his hand, feeling emotionally drained. I let out an exasperated sigh as I thanked him again.

"No need to thank me. It is my job. Your son is a special kid. God bless the two of you for being in his life," the counselor responded while shaking my hand.

I drove home in a daze. He is by far been the most behaviorally challenging kid that we have ever had in our home. However, he was my son and I was up for the challenge. I knew I could handle anything that came my way and that confidence anchored me.

We fostered our son and his older brother for about a year before the adoption went through and their names legally changed to Goodson. One day, the following summer, we went to the pharmacy to refill our son's medicine but the pharmacist was unable to fill the prescription because his last name had changed and the pharmacy didn't have his new name on file. It would take weeks to sort out the paperwork out, but he was on summer break and my wife and I thought that this would be a good time to ween him off of his medicine. Stacey and I were firm believers in not over medicating kids, besides, he was doing well academically and we believed that his medications were no longer needed. Boy, were we wrong.

Our son struggled socially and had a hard time keeping friends. I started noticing a lot of the behaviors that the counselor spoke about in the meeting. He went to a friend's house to have a sleepover and he came home in the middle of the night extremely anxious, and somewhat agitated. He struggled to attach to people, especially his friends. He became extremely defiant and he would argue with us about any and everything. After summer break, school started and his grades started to slip almost immediately. The teachers would tell us that he was being disruptive in class and that he struggled to stay on task. The further his grades slipped, and the more defiant he became, the more I yelled. Through all of this, our son's anxiety went through the roof. All of his diagnoses were prevalent. All of those diagnosed letters were mixed together like alphabet soup but now, the letters appeared to be recognizable.

Realizing that we had made a mistake, Stacey and I sat our son down and tried to have a conversation with him to put him back on his medication. He was reluctant, but eventually agreed to go back on them. That lasted for about four days. On the fifth day, our son had figured out that he did not like the way the meds made him feel. He said that, "the medicine made me calm, and slows me down." He was no longer the center of attention with his peers or the teachers when he took his medicine. The constant disruption at school was his way of getting the attention that he was seeking.

After this realization, we couldn't get him to take his meds anymore. We would find the medicine in the seat pockets in the back of the van after he pretended to take them. It was his freshman year of high school. That year, he failed three classes and had to attend summer school in order to pass and move into the tenth grade. To this day, he still will not take his meds and school is a constant struggle.

But it hasn't been all bad. Our son has been able to attach and make friends. He has meaningful relationships with his peers. He was able to find his way back on to the football team. Going off of his medication made him feel real. He is a charismatic, funny and charming young man and I wouldn't trade him for anyone.

Spoken words of a Foster Dad

One day, I tried to think about the day and the life of a thirteen-year-old boy with multiple diagnoses. In my best attempt at empathy:

Alphabet Soup

You down with ADD? Yeah you know me.
You down with ADD? Yeah you know me.
Who's down with ADD?

Well almost every foster child,
And we can add the hyper for those kids that like to get wild.
Attention Deficit Disorder,
They say I can't even pay attention with quarter.
25cents, and what the doctors keep telling me is making no sense,
Please put away the charts, if they only knew that I had smarts,
And that I am far from dense.
I wasn't acting...it's just the girl....I'm not overreacting
Ooooweee, the girl that was sitting next to me, is distracting.
This time I'll be at my best,
I just need another shot at that test.
I can show you all that I have skills, I'm not faking,
But these pills I'm taking, every morning got me shaking...
ALL I NEED IS ANOTHER CHANCE...
I promise to do better just as soon as I pop this Vyvanse.

Who's down with ADD? Me!
Did I forget to mention,
ADD is a Deficit that experts call a Disorder in order for me to pay attention,
Or not...SQUIRREL!
The test just started but I can't stop looking at that girl.

I NEED YOU TO GET BACK IN YOUR SEAT!
GET BACK IN YOUR SEAT.
Why is it that everyone keeps yelling at me?
Candy Crush on my smartphone, ohh I should try it,
Why does everyone keep telling me that I am defiant?
I'm a kid not a client.

From my position....
Everyone in this school is my opposition.
Me against the world...SQUIRREL...
I can't stop looking at the girl.
Thinking to myself, I'd like to meet her,
As I finally acknowledge the teacher.

Who's down with ODD? Yeah you know me!
Who's down with ODD? Me!
I heard the teacher tell the other teacher that I have ODD...
WRONG JERK FACE...its ADD...get it right!
Oppositional Defiant Disorder...
I haven't heard that one before.
It's new to me...why can't I find a family that'll be true to me?
I'm scared all the time and I'm afraid of what my new dad will do to
me.

This test started 10 minutes ago and I'm only on number 4...
I can't sit still and I'm hard for the teacher to ignore,
Thoughts racing a mile a minute, as I stare at the floor.
PAY ATTENTION! Chirps the teacher. I look up and smile away,
Mind somewhere a mile away.
I'm defiant remember??? I'm not doing this work anyway,
Take out my phone and pretend to dial away.
I wish I had something that would combat it all...
I guess I do yet in still, it's in the form of a pill...
Something called Adderall.

I overheard my Mom tell my Dad,
That I had something called RAD,
All the shuffled letters are making me mad.
They took the letters of the alphabet soup and shook it up...
I still didn't know what RAD meant so I decided to look it up.
RAD develops when a child's most basic needs for nurturing,
Affection, and comfort have not been met." What? No affection?
My big brother held me when I cried? He gave me my protection?

Now all the teachers at school think that I am BAD,
Because I have another damn disorder, something called RAD.
They also said that I can't keep friends...
Pahleese...I had 4 girlfriends in 2 weeks...Meg, Jessica, Kylie, and
Jen.

Who's down with ADD? Yeah you know me...SQUIRREL...
I can't stop looking at that girl. Still not done with this test.
Thinking I don't have a chance at all, wait I do...
Let me pop this Vyvanse and Adderall.
Let's see how they REACT, to this DISORDER,
I'll draw a bubble silhouette of this girl that
I can't get out of my head and ATTACH, to this test...
That way they will know that I just messed, on this multiple guess.
PTSD, I wasn't in a war but I am fighting a losing battle with being
stressed,
PPD, I haven't left the house in 4 days and now they say I'm
depressed.

And what the hell is an IEP? Special Education?
Someone owes me an explanation.
I need someone I can trust...
Glad they got rid of the short bus.

An Individual Education Plan.
I need someone to listen to my plan.
I SAID I NEED SOMEONE TO LISTEN TO MY PLAN!
BILININGINGRIINNNGGGRINGRING sounds the bell.
What the hell? Not yet...I didn't finish my test....
Not again...they will think that I didn't try my best.

Luckily for me, according to my IEP,
I am special enough to have the test read to me.
I'll get another chance, this wasn't my last stance,
At my notes I'll have to glance...
And this time I'll remember to take my Vyvanse.
But that girl in them tight pants tho....SQUIRREL.
SnapChat, another selfie, walking through the halls and the maze of
smartphones...excuse me ma'am, as another pic is posted to
Instagram.
Its only 4th hour and this next class is hard.
Pose...another selfie,
There she is...the girl that I like....maybe she will help me.

Thoughts of a Foster Dad: Key Beliefs and Takeaways

- A full disclosure meeting is very emotional. Prepare for that going into the meeting. You will hear every recorded, horrific detail that happened to your kid. Ask lots of questions to try to gain clarity.
- Education! Education! Education! Learn everything that you possibly can about your kid's diagnosis. Study it! Talk to someone that has a child with the same diagnoses. If possible. Swap stories. Knowing what your child is going through is half the battle. Familiarity is a good thing. It doesn't have to be lonely.
- You are your kid's biggest advocate. As the parent, you'll know best the needs for the child. However, trained professionals will help you make informed decisions.
- When dealing with a kid that has an IEP (Individualized Education Plan), advocate endlessly until you have complete buy in and action from all involved in your child's life. There are professionals both in and out of school that will work with you to put the best plan in place for the child. It is the law for them to follow the plan.
- Get educated on the different medicines that your kid is taking. Understand why they are taking them and what the potential risks and side effects are. As the parent and caregiver, you are the one that will be able to gauge your kid the best. If meds need to be adjusted, then your voice should be heard, especially if you've educated yourself.

The number of teenagers that are in the foster care system that take meds are staggering. Did you know?

- "21 to 39% of children in foster care receive a prescription for psychotropic medication compared with 5 to 10% of children not in foster care."

Chapter 11: I Wanna Go Home!

The numbers are scary

As of 2013, there are 14,615 children in foster care in Michigan; 44% of these children are returned home within 12 months.

Spoken words of a Foster Dad

Winter 2014

Through the eyes of a scared, fourteen-year-old boy, stuck in a residential facility...and all he wants to do is go home. I imagine his misery in this poem:

14 and Black

Man how did I get here? At a place called Kids First. Really? Kids First? If kids were put first then why didn't anyone ask what I want? Kids First is the worst, staff yelling and trippin', the kid next door got caught slippin'...really, trying to steal her purse? Tears are swelling up about to burst, thoughts of my Granny in the back of a black hearse. Man how did I get here? Tears? Nah getting over this hump, I swallow that lump. Evil in my conscious, predator's perpin; staff lurking, like I'm on a watch list. Saltwater dampens my face, damn I hate this place, and on the back of my hand lies waste, of smeared tears.

I can't let them see me cry. Why? I'm 14...I'm a man. Fear, yeah I'm scared as hell and the boys in here, can smell fear, can't give in to peers, because the pressure on the back of my neck is closer than it appears, I want to disappear, but I can't because that punk ass staff member keep staring. What the #$%@ are you looking at? My inner Debo is screaming what the @#$% are you staring at!? I am just strong enough to crush a grape. In my head I am superman with a cape. Its day three, is there anyone coming to get me? If this is Kids First why don't I feel free?

I over-heard the staff talkin', clear words over the other kids squawkin', about this and that...did I just hear him right?...did he just say that BLACK...teenagers are hard to place? Hard to place? I bet he won't say that shit to my face. I hear them talkin' but they are about to see me walkin'. What they mean hard to place? He clearly didn't know that I had 300 plus at my family reunion, I have a uncle that live on a street called Union and he married to my Auntie Susan, my family is inappropriate is what staff is accusin' and and and ....and any day now they'll be here to get me.

I don't care what that staff said, but why can't I get 14 and black out of my head...I remember...I remember the staff member, that said that 14 and black and being a black teenager was like being a member?...a member of what? A member of a gang, a member of a club, a member of a fraternity? I got this fire burning in me, and all I can remember is my Granny in that damn coffin, I hope that this feeling don't happen often. I AM A MEMBER OF MY FAMILY...but why? Why isn't my family...here...paralyzed with fear?

I'm falling Timmmmmbeeeerrrr, and still I remember…the shoveled dirt on her coffin. How did I get here? Its day four, and I don't know if I can take anymore. Thinkin… seeing all of my uncles drinkin, watching the Henny pour, brown liquor hits the floor, poured out for lives lost, but don't my fam realize? I am lost! I get a visit from this white lady, and at this point Kids First is rather shady. Really? She wants me to go home with her? She has a black husband. Her other kids are black…this might be ok. She don't even know me.

I'll do anything to get out of here, so I'll appear, to be sincere, so yes white lady you smell nice, please take me home with you. Kid First? This feels like jail, I just had to do my bid first. In our meeting I'll smile, knowing all the while, I am just biding my time for my family to come and get me, and then it hit me….meanwhile.

What a disgrace…that I am willing to risk what feels like danger with a complete stranger just to escape this place? All I can remember is that punk-ass staff member, that uttered those unforgettable words…"black teenagers are hard to place". SHIT! Mad enough to spit in his face. WHO IS SUPPOSED TO WANT ME??? At first I couldn't believe it, but now it's easy for me to conceive it. Its day five and I'm stuck at Kids First…14 and I'm black, maybe the staff member really did mean it.

Today I watched a group of trained professionals work together to send a fourteen-year-old boy home to a known long-term drug user. When I say it out loud, it sounds horrible, but as I look at it through the lens of a foster dad, it began to become clear. You have to look at the whole picture of a foster child's life to understand that sometimes, there are going to be moments like this.

April 2014

Carter was removed from his home after a well-documented CPS case proved his mom was unfit to parent due to excessive drug use. Upon taking placement of Carter, we noticed right away that he did not take well to having rules and it became very apparent that he marched to the beat of his own drum. Basically, at his house, he had been allowed to do whatever he wanted. Following the rules of our home and his school were extremely challenging for him to accomplish after years of "free-range."

On the second day at our home, he was suspended from school for misuse of a teacher's smartphone. His teacher tried everything to motivate him to do his work so she would reward him for completing mundane tasks by letting him use her phone. He thought it would be funny to go on her personal Facebook page and post a picture of him and his friend with the caption that read, "HANGING WIT MY NIGGAS." This actually showed up on her timeline! For what seemed like hours, her family, friends, peers, and coworkers all saw this post, all frantically attempted to get a hold of her at school to find out what was going on. Because of his foolishness, Carter was suspended for three days. He denied doing it even though he was caught red handed and, even when he admitted that he did it, he would deflect and blame someone else.

This would be the pattern of how his time with us would go. Nothing would *ever* be his fault.

For the next month we drove him to and from his middle school, about a twenty-minute drive each way, and we knew something had to give. It was too much of a hassle to get him to and from school. We did not trust him to take the bus. We didn't trust him to go to school because if left unsupervised, he would have way too much freedom to wreak havoc on the community. It was close to summer break, but he would be enrolled in summer school to recover credits from failing almost every class. Then, a week into summer school, he was suspended indefinitely. He was accused of grabbing a thirteen year old little girl and pulling her behind some bleachers, in an attempt to dry-hump her.

Still, we didn't give up on him. We transferred him to the middle school to be closer to our home. We wanted him to be a part of our community. There, we had a great rapport established with the staff and teachers. There, we felt as if we could get him on the right path. But he did not want to leave his school and he fought us on every front. Reluctantly, after many fights, he went to the middle school in our community near us.

When he started, everything went well. Carter is a very charming, charismatic, and good-looking kid as well as an athlete. Our goal was to help him to make the basketball team so that he would have something that he loved to do at school. We hoped basketball would encourage him to straighten up and "fly straight." It was a major adjustment for him. Overnight, he went from mom not being around for days with no rules, to two parents in the home with structure, guidance, and discipline. For the first time ever, he had adults in his life that held him accountable for his actions. Carter got through a whole marking period, only receiving one in-house suspension. He amazingly passed all but one of his classes. His efforts earned him academic eligibility to play for the 8th-grade basketball team that he tried out for and made. Stacey and I were slapping each other high-fives. We were so thrilled with his progress.

It wasn't all roses

Carter wanted to go home to his mom and he would do almost anything to get there. Carter became extremely disruptive at school and continued to be unbearable at home. He had some serious impulse issues, seeking chaos at every turn. He craved it. I believe that dysfunction made him feel normal. To him, the more chaos and disorder the better. Extreme chaos is what he was used to.

During his search for chaos, he would intentionally antagonize Michael, our oldest adopted son. Carter would physically antagonize Michael by constantly being in his face and poking him. He would verbally assault Michael in an attempt to bully him as well as the other kids in our home. Stacey and I called it "poking the bear." Michael is five foot nine and two hundred sixty pounds and very capable of pummeling most men, let alone a scrawny teenage boy. Carter is only five foot five and one hundred ten pounds soaking wet.

In our home, we require all kids to do their chores and, in doing so, they earn a weekly allowance. But Carter wouldn't do his chores because he didn't have a reason to do them. Carter's mom would give him twenty and fifty dollar bills along with gifts every time he went for a visit. Per the court's instructions, he was not allowed to have any contact with his mom, outside of the agency, including phone conversations; but at every visit, his mom would give him a phone to use.

At school, he could not concentrate because of the phone; it was a clear distraction and a problem. He would call her and she would call him whenever they could. He was disruptive to the class and other kids trying to learn. He would often walk out of class and roam the halls. All of his teachers, including counselors and school social workers, wrote a letter to the psychiatrist with a recommendation for ADHD medicine, but his mom had to sign off on it and she wouldn't. It was clear that he needed counseling. My wife and I provided the opportunity for counseling, which made it even clearer that he had ADHD and needed medication.

We couldn't control him or enforce the rules of the court order in our home because his mom would undermine everything we did. To her, we were the enemy and he didn't have to abide by our rules. When mom caught wind that he was talking about her in a counseling session, she put an immediate stop to it because she didn't want to be the topic of his conversations. Because of her, he would never get the help that he so desperately needed.

After a while, his grades started to slip again. He was deemed ineligible for basketball because of poor academics. Carter's motivation to do well in school went down the drain as soon as he was kicked off of the team. That's when I witnessed one of the most disruptive kids ever! He became even more defiant with basketball being off of the table and his antics became contagious. The other boys in our home started to follow suit. Carter made it impossible for Stacey and me to deal with him in our home because ultimately he was driving a wedge into the harmony of our home and took comfort in doing so.

It wasn't all his fault.

I really felt for the kid. Over a three-month stretch he was dealing with a mountain of trauma:

- Being removed from his home and taken to a group home
- Moving into his first foster home
- Being around a strange but new family
- His Grandmother, his only real caretaker passed away
- Out of three hundred-plus family members, not one person stepped up to take him in and care for him
- He missed his friends in his former school and neighborhood

After parenting Carter for as long as we did, it began to weigh on us; he didn't want to be there. His mom didn't help matters with her visible hatred for us. In family team meetings, she would verbally spew nonsense about how we weren't doing a good job with her son and she told everyone in the meeting that he wasn't safe.

"He is threatened by your son Michael," she would say.

We knew that Carter would not be a good fit for us long-term. Not to mention, he didn't want to be there. He had so many other family members that were suitable options. We finally contacted Carter's worker and asked him to start looking for another placement for Carter with possibly a family member; maybe even his father? Earlier in his placement, while Carter was at basketball camp, he came home and told us he had seen his dad. Carter excitingly said, "I saw my dad today. He walked into the gym, said hi and asked me how I was doing."

I was floored. His bio-dad was working in the same community we lived in and didn't know that his son was in foster care. My wife and I didn't feel like our agency had done enough to find him, so I did it myself. While doing some investigating, I was able to find him and made contact, telling him that I was Carter's foster dad. He informed me that no one had ever attempted to contact him. When I asked him if he could take his son he replied, "My current living situation is not set up for me to take Carter at this time." A small piece of me was heartbroken, but the compassionate side of me felt bad for everyone involved.

We had done all that we could for him but we needed more help! We asked repeatedly and it never happened. Carter needed counseling but his mom blocked that. He needed medication but his mom blocked that. He needed group meetings to include his mom but his mom blocked that. Our hands were tied and my wife and I felt that there was nothing more that we could do for Carter. We contacted our agency and formally asked them to search for a new placement or living arrangement for Carter. We were out of options and patience.

The Courts

I sat in the back of the empty courtroom as a hearing began for Carter's mom Priscilla to determine her progress and if he would be sent back home to her or remain in foster care. All parties were present except for Priscilla. It didn't seem to surprise anybody present that she was late to something as important as her court hearing. Ultimately, he could be going home to her, and she wasn't even there.

From the start of the proceedings, it was clear to me that everyone involved wanted Carter to go home to his mom Priscilla including Carter's foster care worker, the prosecuting attorney, child's attorney, and the Judge.

Carter's foster care worker was on the stand and testified, "The Goodson household was the ideal placement for him. They have a loving two-parent home. Stacey and Julian are both active in the community and the school district that Carter attends. Their sons are of the same age as Carter and attend the same school. The Goodsons have done a fantastic job of providing every resource necessary for Carter to succeed. However, Carter has been extremely disruptive and seems to have sabotaged placement. There isn't anything else that the Goodsons can do to help Carter at this time, without mom allowing more services. They have done all that they can."

When asked about Priscilla's progress, Carter's worker further testified that; "Priscilla hasn't had a positive drug screen for the last two screenings. However, she did have a positive test a month prior."

All of a sudden the door to the courtroom flung open and in walked Priscilla. She was an hour late. She walked in and took her seat, oblivious to what was happening. She noticed Stacey and I were in the courtroom and glared at us as if we were the reason for all of her problems.

Carter's caseworker went on with his testimony saying, "Priscilla resides at 123 Burger. She has maintained this address for the entire time Carter was in placement. I have taken a look at a few of her utility bills and they are current. She has section eight housing."

I thought, "Why aren't they asking how Priscilla is providing for her and her family? Did she have a job? How was she paying for everything?" The court continued without asking these important questions.

The worker continued, "Priscilla has completed all of the parenting classes and necessary counseling appointments the court has asked of her. She has also maintained her argument that she has not been using drugs and doesn't understand how she tested positive a month ago."

Per the request of her attorney, they successfully managed to get secondary drug screening testing. I've never seen this done. A thirty-year drug user saying that she isn't using is laughable to me. The fact that she was able to get an outside company to test her in addition to what was already available was nonsense to me. It was a waste of time and money. Tax payer money at that! The additional drug screening was pointless in my opinion.

The worker went on to say, "Based on the current situation, Carter will not be able to continue placement with the Goodsons. He will most likely be sent to a residential facility for boys unless a suitable family member steps up and take placement of him."

In a paraphrased question the Judge asked; "so based on what you are saying, Carter is fourteen- years old and will be hard to place with another foster family? If he is not placed with a family he will end up in a residential facility?"

The worker replied, "Yes, your Honor."

"Do you think that the best thing for Carter is to go back home to his mom?" The Judge asked inquisitively.

"Yes, your Honor I do," Andy responded.

Ten minutes later the decision was made to send Carter home. Priscilla was still staring at us like we had kicked her dog. She was clueless that the Judge just made the decision to send her son back home with her. Her attorney had to explain to her what was happening. The Judge instructed the caseworker to wait for the order so that Carter could go home that evening.

Was that the best decision?

I sat in the back of the courtroom and remained seated while I tried to process what just happened. I was torn. I didn't believe that his mom was anywhere near rehabilitated and stable enough to care for him. He was on his way back to an environment that was failing him, neglecting him, and turning a blind eye to him. He was returning to a place where he didn't have proper supervision and where school didn't matter. No one in his home held him accountable for anything school related, including attendance. School was much more social to him than anything else. He went late every day and was there to kick it with his friends and maybe get a meal. I didn't believe that he was going to receive any discipline, guidance, or accountability. He was heading back to an environment that was going to allow him to "run the streets."

Based on what I saw, he wasn't strong enough to lead himself down the right path. My opinion based on all of the trouble that he got into in our home, his mischief, mayhem, and zero regard for authority was that no one has ever modeled proper behavior to him. Unless someone – a mentor, a coach, a teacher, or a pastor helped him, he was destined to go down a very destructive path. If he knew better, he'd do better. Carter was very well aware of the history of drug abuse with his mom because he had been exposed to it every day of his life and it was normal to him. In spite of his awareness of the family dysfunction, he was willing to go back to it blindly because of his love and loyalty to his mom. The connection to his family was deeply rooted, and who could blame him? It was all he knew. Naturally, he wanted to be with his family.

The Residential Option

As I think about the option of residential, it is equally as scary. A residential facility for teenage boys can sometimes be similar to a juvenile detention center. Even though Carter hadn't broken any laws, it was very possible that incarceration is where he would be headed. His actions displayed that he was one horrific decision away from being arrested. In a lot of ways, a residential system seems to prepare young people for jail. If he went there, he'd be in an environment where violence and breaking rules were a matter of survival. Staff members do what they can to straighten kids out but many of them flood our juvenile justice system. Carter didn't deserve that. No kid in his situation would. He needed a hug, not a smack. Sending him to a residential facility would teach him, subconsciously, that he was a bad kid.

The other option was another foster home. Let's face it, there aren't very many foster families lining up to take black teenage boys. Specifically, there are even fewer black foster families. I could only imagine what would have happened to Carter in another setting such as ours. As a Youth Development Specialist, I work with students like Carter all of the time and as an adoption and foster care worker, Stacey works with students like Carter as well. We provide what our agency refers to as 'treatment foster care' in our home. We know the system in and out and how to navigate it. I could only imagine if Carter would've ended up in a rural place and not an urban setting. He'd probably run away from the foster home.

He was already a serious challenge for a family that was well equipped to meet his needs, socially and culturally. If you think the number of black fathers that are present in their children's lives, outside of the foster care system are low, then take a look at the ratio of black teenagers that need placement to the available black foster dad. It's embarrassing there are not more black men stepping up to be foster parents. Proper placements are important. In an ideal world, black teenage boys would go with black families. An improper placement can cause a family fatigue, which can lead to burn out. There are not enough foster families, of any race.

I can't help but wonder if money played a factor in the decision. It takes "boatloads" of money to put a kid in a residential facility. It also cost a lot of money to keep a kid in foster care. But who am I to question the motives of trained professionals? I care for Carter and I don't want to see him get hurt. However, I do know this. Carter wanted to go home and Carter was going to be a thorn in the side of any caregiver until he was allowed to go home. I wonder if the professional decision makers that sent Carter back home to his mom are afraid of him getting hurt. The worst-case-scenario scares me to this very day.

Thoughts of a Foster Dad: Key Beliefs and Takeaways

- Beware of what I call, "Family Fatigue." A challenging child can wear on the entire family. The family support system can be affected as well. Recognizing family fatigue is important because you can take all the necessary steps to self-care, yet it can still happen. It is imperative to know when enough is enough.

- Advice to agencies: try not to burn out your families. Have meaningful conversations with them, addressing their concerns, wants, and needs. Listen to them. Families are aware that there are desperate times that call for desperate measures. However, if family fatigue is present, then the placement can have a less than favorable outcome.

- Almost every kid that has come into our home has wanted to go back to their family. If reunification is an option, then help them return home. Your skin can never be thick enough when dealing with the child's biological family. You enter their lives at the most difficult time.

- With structure, love, and understanding, a foster kid can thrive.

I often play a game of "I wonder"

- I wonder if the fatigue of keeping a difficult case on the books and on a caseload played a factor in the child welfare professional's decision to send Carter home.

- I wonder if they made the decision to spare a willing foster family, "family fatigue" so they can then come back and lean on them for later placements.

- If the worst-case scenario played out. If Carter somehow got hurt when he was sent back to his mom's care, I often wonder if careers would be on the line if that happened.

Chapter 12

Mini Me...The Bio Kid

Believe me when I say it, "I love them all as if they are my own, because they are." But I'd be lying if I said that I treated them all the same. I have to treat them different because they are all different.
~ Julian Goodson

Spring 2013

On Sunday morning at the Wyoming Campus of Kentwood Community Church, the pastor announced that it was time collect tithes and offering. The congregation erupted in applause as did I (God loves a cheerful giver). Sitting next to me, my thirteen-year-old son, Gunnor, was clapping right along with me. As the collection plate came around, I reached in my pocket and pulled out a twenty-dollar bill and dropped it in the plate. I glanced over at Gunnor. He reached in his pocket and also put a twenty-dollar bill in the plate. I whispered to him, "Gunz why'd you do that?" He said, "I have everything that I need because of you. Besides, God needs it more than I do." It was one of the proudest moments that I've ever had as a father.

One of the hardest things about being a foster dad is that I don't have a history with the kid that comes into my home. There isn't a historical database to tap into when it comes to parenting them. There is a 'getting to know' period that comes with taking a foster kid into your home that can take months to play out. Foster parents are getting to know a kid on the fly, all while helping him or her deal with the ramifications of abuse that they have endured prior to coming into your home.

However, with Gunnor and Julia there *is* history. I held Gunnor at birth, comforted him when he cried, fed him when was hungry, and disciplined him when he was out of line. I was the first person he saw when he woke up and the last person he saw when he went to bed for the first three years of his life. The foundation that was set is now almost unbreakable. I am his hero and his father; it is the most gratifying job that I will ever have in my lifetime.

Upon my divorce from his mom Mandy, he moved to Phoenix. That is when I saw his resilience. He had a remarkable strength about him, but I always wondered if he just rolled with the punches because he didn't know any better? I guess I'll never know.

Outside of phone calls, text messages, and Skype calls I only see Gunnor when he is not in school. For us, it seems like both Thanksgiving and Christmas breaks are the shortest days of the year. Despite how fast time flies, I love getting to share him with the entire extended family, doing holiday traditions. Spring Break is an intense week-long one-on-one session because my other kids are in school. Six weeks in the summer time is probably the most meaningful because it's the longest amount of time that we get. I only see him for approximately nine weeks a year. However, it is amazing how much of an influence that I have on his life, in the little time that I spend with him. Both of us make sure that we take full advantage of the time that we get with each other and I do believe that we appreciate it more.

Mini Me

One day Stacey barked at Gunnor and he responded just like I would. What made that so odd was that he had never physically seen me react in any way to her.

Stacey said, "Dang boy, you act just like your dad."

"That's because I am a young Junior in Training," he proudly responded.

He looks, talks like me, walks, runs, dribbles, and shoots like me. It is like looking at a younger me in the mirror but even better. With him, it is as if I can control and/or program a younger version of myself. I've always known the importance of being a father but that moment at church was powerful. I felt like I was a superhero and I had special powers. At that moment I really felt like I could change the world and I could do it through him. My son. He is the key. He was watching and copying my every move. He was emulating and acting out my every thought. That changed the game. I must use my special powers for good and not evil. To do this, I have to be the best man that I can be, not part time or not when it's convenient but all the time!

After that powerful moment in church, I started to pay attention. I became mindfully observant of how my other sons viewed me. Did they look up to me with that same sense of intensity? Next thing I noticed was that Dre' was dressing like me. I noticed Michael using my hand gestures. I noticed Jason's speech and wordplay start to emulate my own. I even observed Derek, one of Dre's friends, use one of my phrases that I would say to Stacey, as he was talking to his girlfriend. I thought it was different with Gunnor because he was biologically mine and he looked the part. I'm sure some of it is hereditary, but I'm positive that is not all of it; environment matters too.

Expectations!

Chris Sain Jr, author of the book *"Dumb Athlete,"* delivered a powerful motivational message to a group of young teenage males that I was mentoring. Chris explained to them that they should "become a product of their expectations and not their environment." Since I heard him deliver this message to those kids, I have changed the way that I motivate kids that I parent. I now ask my kids what they expect and every one of them has a different response. Every one of our foster care children comes from a background of abuse, neglect and abandonment. They may have all had abuse and neglect in common, but their environments prior to living with me were very different. Therefore, each one of their expectations of themselves are different. Now, every day at some point of the day I ask one of my kids, "What are your expectations for today?" Upon an answer, I'd respond by saying, "ok, how will you get there?" I don't expect an answer. The whole conversation is to get them to think about how they will go about achieving their goals for the day. My hope is to instill positive habits in them. I want to get them to think about much more than what they will wear to school that day.

This experience has taught me that I also had to curb my expectations.

As a parent, one of the biggest things we use to measure success is school outcomes. How is their behavior at school and in the community? How well are they doing academically?

Parents, do you sometimes live and die by the grades that your kids receive at school? I did.

I expected Julia to graduate from high school and she did. I expect Gunnor to one day graduate from high school. Expecting the other kids in my home to do the same may be an unfair expectation that I put on them. Same goes for their behaviors and their athleticism. Just because we are a basketball playing family doesn't mean that all of them can hoop. Curbing my expectations is hard because I had some success with my biological kids. Julia was accepted into Arizona State University and was an all-state track athlete. Gunnor is currently carrying a 3.8 grade point average and is very good at basketball. My parenting style is working for them because I had history with them. With the help of their mom, we were able to mold them and instill good habits at a young age. I don't have that luxury with my other children so I have to take a different approach. The formula that I used for one kid may not or will not work for the next one. The last thing that I want to do is compare the two. The quickest way to drive a wedge between kids is to compare them. I could never tell Dre' to be more like Gunnor. However, I can encourage Julia to help Dre' along in an encouraging way, and that goes for much more than academics! She needs to help Dre' along as it pertains to the #TeamGoodson way of doing things. Gunnor will teach his brothers what it means to be a Goodson and to honor the name.

Coaching as an advantage

Another thing that I took away from Chris Sain's book, "*Dumb Athlete*" was his take on being the star athlete. Chris explained that "because he was often the star of his team, he was neglected by his coaches." As a coach I have been guilty of this. I have also been guilty of this as a dad. On the playing field your star athlete typically doesn't need the same attention from the coach as kids with average or lesser talent do. As a coach I have diverted my attention to the kids that needed my attention the most so that I could get their skill set to match the star player. But what if I spent that same amount of time with the star player as I did with the weaker ones? Would my star player turn into a greater player? Would my star player reach his ultimate potential? Would my star player become a leader? A kid is more likely to reach his potential if you have invested the proper time in him. Gunnor is off to an awesome start and will continue to excel. My job as a father is to make sure that I am continuing to help him to reach his potential. I just have to be mindful to give Gunnor the time that he deserves. Gunnor may be the youngest but he is the leader in the pecking order amongst his brothers; they look up to him.

When Stacey and I decided to answer God's calling for us to become foster care and adoptive parents, we sat both Julia and Gunnor down and had a family discussion. Both kids loved the idea of doing it. Julia is naturally compassionate about helping others and Gunnor liked the idea of having some brothers around. When Gunnor goes home to his mom in Phoenix, he is an only child. He gets all of her attention. When he is with us, his brothers are around and there is always someone for him to be a kid with. Gunnor's mom and I are making the best of our situations. It's not what we planned but Gunnor is truly receiving the best of both worlds.

Spoken words of a Foster Dad

Summer 2012

This is for the dad's out there forced into a Co-Parenting role! You may only have your son part-time, you still have to be a full-time parent. Just remember to hug your child and keep it moving. A letter to Gunnor!

From Me to You

Two weeks old staring down at my baby boy excitedly scared, I don't know if you felt me, but God answered my prayers and made you healthy, my soul I bared, 10 fingers 10 toes is all I cared. My little seed, to be a good dad is not a want it's a need, so forgive me if I preach to you, but from me to you as a man and a dad, there are a few things that I must teach to you.

From me to you take things slow...life is not a track meet, as I selfishly want you to be an athlete. It was me that put the basketball in your bassinette, athletics and education can be driven in this vehicle of life so put your seatbelt on and fasten it. You can lean on me for anything...from me to you I got your protection, I'll give you direction, when you play in that championship game I promise to be the loudest in the parent section.

So, I need you to know, it is a pleasure to watch a little mini me grow. From me to you I'm extremely delighted, how you come to me, eyes wide excited. "Dad, I love bbq ribs." I'll teach you to griddle it! "Dad, I love Hip Hop music." Then we'll listen to Jay-Z riddle it! "Dad, I love basketball." Don't delay, bring the ball to the driveway...I'll teach you how to dribble it!

From me to you, you always have to care, so in the presence of a woman try not to swear. If there is a woman present then pull out the chair. If there is a woman present then hold the door, if you are talking you are not listening, and if you listen to a real woman, you will leave her wanting more. "Dad I want her to like me." She will son, don't give her mean eyes, just look at her with those big green eyes, listen and smile...you are a Goodson, you are a good catch...you have no choice but to have style.

My dad, your PaPa told me that "chicks come dime a dozen, but a real woman lasts a lifetime." So in due time, and if you must, in search of that good lovin', from what you believe to be that good woman, and you feel like your gonna bust, ALWAYS USE A CONDOM, this you have to trust. If you do this every time, you will extend your lifeline! So I advise you to wait for that special girl and when you find it hold on with all your might, Hold on, Hold on, Hold on tight...from me to you, if you treat her right, she will always be by your side and never take flight.

People are going to make you mad, just know, so, before you lose your temper and blow, take a deep breath. Then let they asses have it! Respect is earned not given, Respect is a key ingredient in livin'. Respect those that respect you back, but most importantly respect your family and yourself...from me to you, this is a quality that cannot lack.

I apologize that it didn't work out with me and your mom...it is difficult on everyone to co-parent, I want you with me all the time but you're not and it is hard for me to bear it, but you got two families that love you and it is plenty of you and your love for all of us to share it, I'll do all that I can to take care of it, so from me to you, I'll protect you like body armor, your love is my badge of honor, and as your dad I proudly wear it.

From me to you I got you, I got you when you call, always go hard and if you come up short, I got your support, and I got you when you fall. From me to you know that I always got your back, but if you ever step out of line you will get wacked, so if I ever hear that you slacked, then it is my job to make sure you get smacked...because I love you....I still can't believe it, you're in Phoenix, and I'm in

Michigan, but God can grant my Wish Again, from me to you all you gotta do is give me the word and my bags are packed, as a son needs his father so that his life will stay on track.

Thoughts of a Foster Dad: Key Beliefs and Takeaways

- It is important to have realistic expectations. You can drive yourself crazy trying to get a kid to attain unrealistic expectations, also, it is simply unfair to the child if the parent has unrealistic expectations.
- Set small goals with realistic expectations and remain consistent. Remember that it is not a sprint, it's a marathon. Foster kids will not be able to change overnight and it is unfair to expect them to.
- Because one method of discipline or consequences worked for one kid doesn't mean that it will work for the next one.
- Do not, by any means, assume that your biological kids are fine. Talk to them. Ask them how they are doing with everything; there are a lot of changes to adjust to when adding a new member to the household and family.
- If you have a bio kid in the home with you then please give them the time that they deserve. It is easy to be so consumed with giving your attention to the "squeaky wheel" that you can miss some key teaching moments with your bio kid. Encourage your bio kid to set the example and model the expectations of the rules and the culture of the home.
- We are human. We make mistakes and so do the children. Give yourself grace as well as the children. Expect to make mistakes. Learn from them and make changes to how you do things next time.
- As much as we may want to, we cannot do the work for them. We have to give them the tools necessary to get their schoolwork done. We have to have the patience to help them grow within themselves. Their grades are not a direct result on how well you are doing as a parent. Try not to take it personal. We can set expectations for them and encourage them to try their hardest to reach them. Your

child's mental health and happiness are more important than their grades.

Chapter 13

Breaking Cycles

"Every child that has come into our home has suffered some form of abuse, albeit emotional or physical." ~ Julian Goodson

How do we teach our kids better so that they don't do it to their kids one day? How do we break the cycle?

People often ask us, "Julian, why do you and Stacey take the kids that everyone else has given up on? What motivates you to do that?"

We simply tell them, "Our goal is to show our kids every day what a family structure looks like. Our goal is to show our kids what parents do for their family. If we show them better, then maybe when they have children and families of their own, they will do better. Therefore, breaking the cycle."

Often, kids don't do what you tell them, but they will do what you show them. The day my aunt came to pick me up and took me away from my childhood home on 1010 Eastern, marked the day that I truly believe we broke the cycle. Even though I had been given a strong foundation of a family structure, it didn't go without its dysfunction. I had every opportunity to head down a destructive path. I was well on my way down a very deep hole. My dad did show me a family dynamic and a work ethic. However, he also showed me another side that was filled with illegal drug activity as well as drug use and abuse. I'm positive that his intentions were good, but subconsciously, he had also paved the way for me to do the unthinkable. For me, it would have been very easy to pick up the phone and be the second generation Goodson Kingpin. Instead, I put myself through school and carved out a career. I wouldn't have done that if my aunt hadn't stepped in.

Here is a conversation that I had with my foster daughter Jazmine or "Jazzie," is what we call her:

"Dad, when are you going to whoop Dre'?" Jazzie randomly asked me, as we are sitting on the couch watching a bad episode of "Love and Hip Hop."

"Why would I do that?" I asked with a wrinkled up face.

"Look at how bad he is and how disrespectful he is," Jazzie said.

"Do you not like what he is doing?" I asked.

"I don't like the way that he speaks to both you and mom. He needs to get smacked in his mouth," she blurted.

I asked calmly, "Jazzie do you think that is what he needs? The number one rule in this house is to treat others how you want to be treated. How would you like it if he were to smack you in the mouth? Or if I did it?"

"When I have a kid there is no way that I will allow him to talk to me the way that Dre' talks to you. I'd take off my belt. That's how my dad did it to me and my sister. So, that is what should be done to him," she said to me in a frustrated tone.

Standing to turn off the television, I turned to speak to her, "Jazzie there are other ways to discipline your child. Physically harming a child is not a good idea in my opinion. So let me ask you this. You and your sister were removed from your dad for him hitting you inappropriately. Was your dad wrong when he hit you like that?"

Silence...turn into tears. Jazzie was now wiping her face.

Consoling her with a hug, I let go of her embrace and continued, "Jazzie it is my job to teach you the right way to resolve problems and conflict. It is my job to teach you how to communicate. You will learn how to love unconditionally, so that one day, you don't teach your kids the same physical abuse that has been taught to you."

Jazzie didn't know that it was wrong to hit her child, because that is all she knew. It's what her dad demonstrated. She didn't know any better. Until she came to live with us, being beaten was a way of life. Spanking your child was how you received the desired results from a child. Hopefully, my parenting style and the way that my wife and I manage our household will show her a different way of doing things. If we model proper parenting then so will they.

There are generations of families that have loved ones who end up in foster care.

Comparatively, generations of families endure welfare and poverty. Often, if a kid ends up in the child welfare system, then the chances of that same kid one-day having children that spend some time in the welfare system are significantly higher. In order to break the cycle, a child will need more than luck or circumstance. Some people are a result of their environment. When it comes to foster care, nothing can be further from the truth. Foster care isn't a black thing or a white thing. It isn't a poor thing or a rich thing. It's about abuse and neglect! Foster care is about trauma.

Foster care has no discrimination and breaking the cycle has to be done deliberately. There is a paradigm shift that takes place. Wanting to do something and knowing how to do something are two totally different things. Let's take Julia's mom, Janine's situation for example. She never had anyone that took her under their wing. No one showed her how to change her habits or form positive ones. Janine was unable to create a new culture that included love, guidance, understanding, and patience. Because she never received it, she was never able to model those learned behaviors to her kids. Did she want love, guidance, and understanding, for her own children? Of course, she did. Janine went on to have two more kids. Out of all four her kids that she gave birth to, she lost custody of two of them. That's not a coincidence.

For some foster kids, it is a matter of simply showing them better. They will come into your home with their own preconceived notions as to how their perfect family will look. Some will flourish in your home because of the love, guidance, and safety they receive.

Kids thrive with proper structure. Others will never see your family structure as a perfect one because some key components are missing such as their biological parents and siblings. As foster parents, all we can do is show them what our beliefs of a family look like. My wife and I are very intentional about it.

Take my situation of moving in with my Aunt, Uncle and cousins for instance. I established a brotherly bond with my cousins right away. That was very deliberate both on my part and the part of my Aunt and Uncle. It was important for me to a have a sense of belonging and normalcy. Because they did that, I felt that I belonged. I was one of them. A family member. I was family, even though I possessed a different last name.

When a kid comes into my home, I immediately introduce them to my kids as brother and sister. My hope is that subconsciously or consciously, something resonates within that child to have a sibling relationship instead of a foster one. For reasons that I have yet to completely figure out, the kids in our home are very close and remain close even after they leave. I believe that is a direct result of how they are introduced, as well as being treated the same as every other kid living in the home. My aunt not only helped break the cycle of my destructive path, she also broke the cycle of what could have been a broken family structure. She replaced my ideas of what family was. It didn't have to be traditional. Just because I was her nephew it didn't mean that I wasn't treated the same as my cousins. Just because they were my cousins didn't mean that I couldn't treat them like brothers and sisters. Her actions affirmed my now beliefs of, "family is what you make it." I learned that from her and still treasure it to this day.

Thoughts of a Foster Dad: Key Beliefs and Takeaways

- When bringing a kid into your home, consider introducing them to the other kids in your home as their brother or sister. Oftentimes, kids already have the foster care system in common, so they will naturally have a connection in most cases.
- Cultivating healthy habits right away is very important. Kids are not going to change their way of thinking overnight. If you go into it trying to change them and their way of thinking it will backfire. All we can do is plant seeds. We have to show them good behaviors and not just speak them.
- Kids have to know that you care before they care what you think. We may think that we know what they need and try to give it to them without even asking what they want. Giving them healthy choices, while helping them to make informed decisions, is one way for the cycle to be broken.

Chapter 14

On My Own But Not Alone

If education is the key to success, then foster care kids that age out of the system face the biggest challenge of unlocking the door to their true potential. Did you know?

Youth formerly in foster care are three times more likely to not have a high school diploma or GED than youth not formerly in foster care.

Youth formerly in foster care are one fifth less likely to have a college degree than youth not formerly in foster care.

Less than 3% of foster youth that age out of the system go to college.

After my wife and I got acclimated to having Michael and Andre in our home, things were settling into a nice, normal routine - about as normal as one could imagine under the circumstances. We began to ponder the idea of taking on another foster child. This time, for some odd reason, we were somewhat picky. We liked the idea of adding a young girl to our household to add some balance. Maybe right around the ages of six to ten years old. We prayed on it. We went a couple of weeks before we told our worker what we would be interested in trying next. The phone finally rang. It was our foster care worker asking us to take a seventeen-year-old young man for the weekend or what she would call respite. That's when I was humbled. God has an incredible sense of humor. Shame on me for being specific in what I was being called by God to do. It started out as a weekend, which turned into two weeks, then turned into two months, and finally turned into a permanent placement. Darrin was his name. D was what we called him. He was seventeen years old but his appearance made him look like a grown young man. Standing six feet tall and one hundred seventy-five pounds, broad shoulders, and fashion savvy, D was a very attractive young black man with facial hair. Right away he showed his charm and wit. He displayed a charisma for speaking to people. He showed incredible drive and independence and it was quite refreshing because the other boys didn't possess those qualities. After he settled in, I sat him down and explained to him the house rules. I also helped him identify some of the short-term goals that he wanted to accomplish. The Goodson Family Rules are simple and as follows:

- Treat others how you want to be treated
- Always give 100% in everything that you do
- Everyone is a part of this family and will be treated as such

I explained to him that everyone has to pull their weight and doing daily chores were expected. D was very motivated by money. He has a work ethic and a hustle about him that I have yet to witness again in a seventeen-year-old. He already had a job at Spectrum Health Hospital which was equally impressive. Michael and Dre' looked up to him because of his job and how he talked about it. I was hoping to look to him for some peer-to-peer role-modeling. However, his senior year in high school, D struggled with doing the work. Not that he was incapable. School just wasn't his focus. I was determined to see him graduate. I also explained to him that if he was to stay with us then he had to conform to a family structure – a mom, dad, and siblings. When we have family events and outings, then he would be expected to participate if his schedule allowed. He agreed.

D was in our house for a couple of months and then the honeymoon period was over! He became defiant, disruptive and disobedient. He had ZERO desire to follow the rules and did not feel as though they applied to him. In my opinion, he started to like us and that scared him to no end. He disobeyed our rules in what seemed like an effort for us to throw him out. We were D's eleventh and final placement. I truly understood why other foster families gave up and threw in the towel. Still, I was determined to break through and be there for him when everyone else had failed him (to no fault of their own).

Everyone's family has a breaking point.

I found an empty condom wrapper in his room. Now, I have come across condoms before in the house. I knew they were his. I knew that he had a girlfriend so when I saw it the first time we had a sit-down. I told him that I was proud of him for making the decision to be protected. In doing so, he was making grown-up choices and having sex can have some grown-up consequences. It was a great teaching moment. I'm sure that I was the first person to ever have "The Talk" with him. He told me so. However, when I saw the empty wrapper my blood started to boil because I automatically assumed that he had sex in my house. When I confronted him I could tell that I scared him with the booming bass that I had in my voice and the tone that I took. I had to check myself and calm myself down. Surprisingly, he didn't go on the defensive. He convinced me that he would never have sex in my house as he wouldn't disrespect me or Stacey like that. He told me that when he was at his girlfriend's house, he took the empty condom wrapper and stuck it in his pocket. Against my better judgment, I believed him. A couple of days later I woke up in the middle of the night to use the bathroom. I stepped into the kitchen to grab a drink of water and decided to check in on the boys. It was quiet all throughout the house. However, when I checked on D he was nowhere to be found. I knew exactly where he was. I sent him a text message:

"You have thirty minutes to get back here before I lock this door and you won't get back in."

"Oh Shit!" Was his reply.

He was home in fifteen minutes.

That's when I realized that he left my house exposed in the middle of the night just so he could chase some tail. Two days later, my Spidey senses were tingling so I stayed up long enough to check his movements. He literally tried to sneak out while I was still awake. I called him out on it. He then begged me to let him go to his girlfriend's house after midnight.

"Please! Just let me go over there for a minute," D pleaded.

"No!" I replied firmly.

"Why not?" He asked, almost whining.

"For obvious reasons!" I responded firmly.

"Man that's BULLSHIT!" He screamed. "I'm eighteen now, I should just be able to go when I want!" He said boasting.

I stood up and said through clenched teeth, "Hey watch your mouth and your tone!"

"Why won't you just let me go...I'm coming right back." D said, pleading again.

I respond, "There are a handful of reasons why I'm not letting you go."

"I know when you were eighteen you've done exactly what I am trying to do now." Said D, in an attempt to reason.

"Maybe, but we're not talking about me, we are talking about you. I'm the grownup, you're the child." I said, sounding a lot like my Uncle Leroy.

"Man I know, but I'm trying to do 'The Grown Up'." Begged D, displaying a poor attempt at humor, clearly letting me know that he was trying to have sex with his girlfriend.

"When you make a grown-up living and you pay grown-up bills, and you are in your own grown-up house, then you can do "The Grown-Up" all you want. But not in this house and not on my watch." I replied, surprisingly sounding like my dad.

I pressed on, "And you want to know why? You're eighteen she is sixteen. That's statutory rape! I don't condone that. I will not knowingly allow you to disrespect another families' house by letting you sneak in through a window. Have some respect for them. If you can't walk through the front door then you shouldn't be there. If you had a daughter and you knew her boyfriend was literally sneaking into your house to have sex with her what would you do? Imagine you have a house and you saw a black man sneaking in through the window...would you shoot first and ask questions later?

So, sorry if you think I'm being a hard-ass...but from where I stand I am trying to save your life."

"This is some BULLSHIT!!!" D said, walking away from me toward his bedroom.

"YOU GOT ONE MORE TIME TO FIX YOUR MOUTH TO FORM A CURSE WORD AT ME...YOU WILL RESPECT ME IN MY HOUSE!!!!" I screamed in an "I will fight you right now" tone.

"My bad," said D, retreating from my challenging demeanor, while closing the door to his bedroom.

For the next two nights, he was impossible. He was flexing his muscles and trying to establish some type of territory while trying to gain his manhood. He was incredibly defiant. His tone changed from talking to us, to talking at us. There was a noticeable change. He made it very difficult to ignore his shenanigans. The next night it happened again. The other boys looked up to him and noticed that his behavior had become aggressive. It was his attempt to establish himself. It was becoming a problem with the other boys. How was it fair that he had his own set of rules? They started to question me. Then it happened again! This time, D snuck out, I noticed that he left the front door open. Not just unlocked but physically ajar. I was livid. We live on a busy four- lane street in an urban area. He left my house wide open while we slept. Anyone could've walked in my home. My mind automatically went toward protection and at that point, I knew that D had to go. This time, I didn't send him a text message. This time, I shut the door and locked it up. I went back inside and went to bed. It was a little after two o'clock in the morning. At around five thirty in the morning, we heard a loud banging on the door. Stacey got up and let him in. He became very aggressive toward her. His body language appeared to look like he was ready to fight. Later that morning Stacey took the boys to school. She came back and we both decided that a change needed to be made. We called his worker and gave her the news. She didn't take the news well as she had grown quite attached to him. I'm sure she just wanted to see it all work out with us. She was hopeful that we'd be his family. She understood why, however. The conversation with D when he got home from school was a hard one to have.

"Why? Why do I have to leave?" Asked D.

I display a blank stare while trying to formulate my thoughts, I reply "Because it's time."

"Huh?" D responded, but not surprised by my words.

"How many times do you think that I'd let you break the rules? Bad choices have consequences," I explained.

"Just for sneaking out?" He replied sounded wounded.

"It's not just for sneaking out D. You haven't done your chores in months. When we ask you to do anything around here it doesn't get done. I can't have one set of rules for you and another set of rules for the rest of the kids in the house."

"Oh, so now you're putting me out because I won't do the fucking dishes?" Questioned D, in an angry tone.

"No, but that disrespectful tone in which you curse at me and my wife as if we aren't the providers and adults is one of the big reasons. The last thing I am going to let happen in my house is for a kid to disrespect me, my wife or any other family member. If you talked to your boss like that, what do you think would happen?" I said, shaking my head.

I explained further, "You also have to realize that this is a family unit and you buck the rules constantly. I am trying to show you what a family structure looks like so that when you have a family of your own, you will know what to do. I want you to learn how to be a leader so that you can be the head of a household."

"But I am independent and I don't need your help like that." He said, sounding somewhat defeated.

"There you go, constantly biting the hand of the feeder." I responded, now calm and breathing steady.

"Huh?" He responded confused.

In my best "teacher voice" I explained, "You are telling me that you are independent but yet asking if you can stay in my home. Seriously? Make that make sense. I told you from the start, that you had to be a part of a family structure. That was the only way that it would work because of how I run my household. It has structure. And with structure comes rules, responsibilities, and discipline. Discipline lives here. However, you want to treat my house as if it is your own place that you can come, go, and do what you want. This house is not an independent living house. A mom, dad, love, and guidance lives in this home and you don't want any part of that."

"Can I please just stay here until I finish school? I know that I haven't been a part of your family stuff. I just don't want that," Pleads D.

"No!" I said firmly, even though it hurt.

"You said that you wouldn't give up on me." He says, in an emotional meltdown.

I attempted to hug and console him but he pushed me away.

"You you...you" He stuttered and sniffed back tears. "You said that you wouldn't give up on me," he said, composing himself.

Lovingly I told him, "D listen to me! I'm not putting you out. I'm helping you move on. It's a big difference. I'm not saying that you have to go right this minute. I have a heart, and I do care about you. I would never put a child that I cared about out on the street."

"But I still have to go? Every foster home that I have been in has done this." He cried out.

"Not like this! You told me that the last home you were in put your stuff out on the front lawn. That family wouldn't even let you back inside. Did I do that? Your stuff is still in your room." I responded pointing at his room.

D let out a big sigh but gave a blank stare.

I continued, "I'm not putting you out, I am helping you move on. Stacey and I are still going to be a part of your life if you want. I will still help you with your development if you want. I am not giving up on you. I just believe that there is a better way for me to teach you, that doesn't involve you living here. You have been displaying independent living actions, so I am setting you up for independent living. I believe in you. I will help you. I will be there with you every step of the way."

D got up and walked out; his worker was still at the house so the two of them went to the back deck to talk. I went to my room for a minute to gather myself and collect my thoughts. I came out and asked him if he was okay, He replied that he was good. For the next couple of days, D was on his best behavior around the house and at school. The dust had settled, and he was a lot more attentive around the house. I could tell that he was making a conscious effort to be around more. All of a sudden, he showed up at the dinner table. He asked if we could talk. As we sat down he told me that he had started to look at apartments. He pulled out brochures, floor plans, and applications. For the first time since I'd met him, he was asking me for help. I was floored. I knew he had "drive and ambition" but now he was showing maturity. I gave him my advice. He was receptive to me guiding him in this process. He admitted to being scared of going out on his own, but now he understood that it was for the best. I reassured him that he wouldn't be on his own. We'd be close by. Stacey and I will help with whatever he needed.

Over the next week or so I drove him to see a few apartments. He found one that he liked, so I helped him with the application. He needed a reference and I was happy to help. Then it came time to put down the security deposit and first month's rent. Stacey and I were fully prepared to scratch a check to get him started until he said the unthinkable. "I don't need your help! I have saved up enough to pay for it. Thanks, but I need to do this on my own." D had saved a good portion of his money from working all of those hours at the hospital.

He was smart enough to move into an apartment that was a block away from his high school and on the city bus line. Stacey and I helped him turn on his utilities by showing him what to do. We then used our resources to furnish his entire one bedroom apartment. We took him grocery shopping, filled up his fridge, and bought bedding, dishes, and toiletries. D proceeded to go to work and school and we got to see him weekly. Soon thereafter, it became like any other kid that leaves home, coming back for a meal, and to do laundry. He often called when he needed help or a ride home from work. Stacey would often buy groceries and put it in his fridge when he wasn't there. He seemed to be doing quite well, all things considered.

About six months later, I went to the mailbox. It contained something from the school that was addressed to the parent guardian of Darrin Gowin. He asked us to open it for him and, when I did, I was shocked. Inside was his High School Diploma. When D first came to us he was failing almost every class. Although he needed a fifth year of high school, he finished the race and accomplished what many kids in his situation couldn't. Graduation is expected for a lot of teenage kids but, for a foster kid, it is quite the milestone.

Typically, when a foster care youth turns eighteen they are sometimes thrown out of their foster homes. Some families move children out as soon as the checks stop coming in. There have been countless foster kids that had their foster care families put them out days after turning eighteen. I recall one of my son Michael's friends calling us on New Year's Eve asking us to pick him up in the middle of a snow storm because his family had put him out. It was a week after his eighteenth birthday.

Where do they go?

What do they do?

These kids have no family to turn to, no education, no skills, guidance, work, or rental history and, often times, no driver's license. However, they are expected to rise up, and all of a sudden, take care of themselves because they are eighteen. Really? In my experience, foster kids are more likely to be incarcerated. My experience has shown me that foster kids are more likely to have a substance abuse issue. My experience has shown me that girls that spent time in foster care are more likely to become pregnant only months after leaving foster care.

Kids in traditional families have resources that will help them in the next phase of life. Foster kids, however, don't have that luxury. They have very few resources to turn to. So I often wonder about D. What would have happened to him if I just put him out without any support? Would he have graduated? Remained employed? Have a warm apartment with food in the refrigerator?

The day D came to us, his worker told us that he had two options: our family was his first option and going to a residential facility in Detroit was his second. When we allowed him to come and stay with us, I truly believe that we helped break the cycle that day.

As my aunt had done for me as a teenager, I was able to do the same. We paid it forward to another in the same way. One of the best feelings that a foster parent can have is to know that they helped to change the course of a young person's life in a positive way.

The magic number for a foster kid is eighteen. At that point, a foster kid doesn't have to listen to a worker, therapist, mentor, or any more child welfare professionals. In many ways, it is a day that they crave because they are often unable to make any choices in their lives up until that point. No kid chooses to be in foster care. So for many, the first chance they get, they elect to go out on their own. Here in Michigan, upon turning eighteen, a kid can elect to go back into the foster care system up until they are twenty-one years of age and there are advantages to doing so. A kid will still have resources like case management, a monthly stipend, coverage for medical, and education expenses.

In D's case, this was perfect because he didn't want to be adopted, nor did he want guardianship, or anyone telling him what he could or couldn't do. However, he learned to use us as a support system properly, so that he could get his needs met. Today, D is now nineteen years old and doing very well by most adult standards. He has his own apartment. He has a full-time job as a security guard. He is a full-time college student at Grand Rapids Community College pursuing his dream of a degree in Criminal Justice. His goal is to one day be a Police Officer. It is much easier to do well by societies standards when your basic housing needs are met.

D is very much a part of our family unit. He is with us just like any other nineteen years old that went away to college. He comes for birthdays, cookouts, holidays, to get a meal, and to do laundry. He'll call me when he needs advice or just wants to talk. He will also call me when he needs help. As much as he bucked our house and our rules, he came to appreciate the love, guidance, and stability that we shared with him. The biggest compliment he recently gave us was to my wife Stacey. He said, "Stacey before I get married, my girl has to come over here to learn from you. She has to go through mother-wife boot camp." I am very happy that I handled things the way that I did. I didn't cast away an angry and confused teenager. I gained a son. He may be on his own, but he is not alone.

Thoughts of a Foster Dad: Key Beliefs and Takeaways

- Family! Family! Family! Although D claimed to not want to be a part of our traditional family unit, it didn't mean that he didn't need one.
- Just because a kid turns eighteen doesn't mean he or she is an adult. They have to be taught how to live on their own. Most importantly, they need a support system.
- Foster kids turning eighteen are a very underserviced demographic and something must be done to provide not only housing, but assistance along the way. It is scary to me what happens to D if we don't walk alongside him in his journey.
- Help kids to know the laws of their state and all the available resources that may be available to them. Help them make the right decision but most importantly, support their decision as the adult that they are trying to become.
- It is much easier to concentrate on doing better for yourself when you are not worrying about where you will sleep at night or where your next meal will come from. Add a support system and some love, and a boy can become a young man.
- As a foster dad I still had to maintain the discipline, structure, integrity, and protection of the home. Nothing could compromise it. Despite the needs of an eighteen-year-old, tough decisions needed to be made to protect everyone involved, including myself.

It's in the numbers

- Almost one quarter of youth formerly in foster care have experienced homelessness.

- In any given year, foster children make up less than 0.3% of the state's population, and yet 40% of persons living in homeless shelters are former foster children.
- 65% of foster youth that age out of the system emancipate without a place to live.
- 51% of foster youth that age out of the system are unemployed.

"Thoughts of a Foster Dad" Thanks and Acknowledgements

I want to thank my Lord and Savior Jesus Christ for whom I've learned to love more and more each day. None of it would be possible without God Almighty. I want to thank my loving wife Stacey Goodson for all of the support. I appreciate the countless conversations and you listening to my random thoughts and rants that I'd make. Thank you for putting up with me, as I pecked away at the keyboard and zoned out into writing land. You are truly my better half. Tiffany Clarke! You were much more of a therapist than an editor. I am forever indebted to you. To Kristen Myers-Chatman, thank you for editing my work. Because of you, my tenses make sense. The periods and the commas are in the right places and spaces. I want to thank #TheProgram. Let's see if I can get this right on the first try. Julia, D, Jazmine, Michael, Dre', Derrick, Steph, Jason, Melvin, Gunnor??? I'm sure there will be one more kid to add to the list before this book goes to print. I want to thank my fellow Foster and Adoptive Dads, Darryl Kirkland, Cole Williams and Steve Tiemeyer. Chopping it up with you guys helps me in more ways that you can imagine. You guys truly understand what I'm going through and I value the talks that we have. Thanks to the Director of Grand Rapids Center for Community Transformation, Justin Beene. Justin, you hired me to be a Youth Development Specialist for the Center, specializing in teaching foster care youth employability skills. I thank you for giving me a shot when no one else would. Shout out to Trauma Specialist, Liz Sharda. I couldn't have put my thoughts on the importance of my own trauma into words without you. Thanks to Gwen Heatley for allowing me a seat on the board for On My Own. On My Own is a non-profit that advocates for youth that will age out of the foster-care system. WE

NEED HELP AND HOMES PEOPLE! Special thanks to Christopher Hall. I know you wanted me to run for the Wyoming Public School Board. God had another campaign for you to manage called "Thoughts of a Foster Dad."

Thank you to the best in-laws ever. My sisters from another mister, Brenda and Julie. My mom Kathy Bergakker. Shout out to my sisters holding down their families as well as their men... Gwen, Cindy and Tracey. Thank you to the best role models a man can have in my big brother Derek Goodson (who successfully put two girls through college), and my Father-in-law Curt Bergakker. You two are superstar fathers. I have to thank my Aunt and Uncle, Leroy and Carol Davis. RIP Uncle Leroy. I truly don't know where my life would be without you two. You two are the direct reason that I go as hard as I do for foster kids. Thanks to my cousins Ryan, Marcus, and Mel Davis. Love you all. Thanks for loving me like a brother. Shout out to my Ottawa Hills High School class of 90 friends. Lyonel, Lynee, Anika, Tyreece, William, Nikki, Josette, Shannon, Lacy...our class was special and you guys set the bar super high. I'm just trying to keep up. Indians for Life! Special shout out to Buster Buscat Eddie Lee Laird!!! I love you bruh. I know I can always count on you to answer the phone when I need you to. Thanks to my MorrGood Family...Greg Morris, Laura Merritt and my brother from another mother Eric Brown. Thanks to the Urban Boss himself Suryia Davenport...you are an inspiration to many. Anthony Lambers, the world needs to hear your story. I hope my story will inspire you to tell yours. Thank you. Keep up the good work with our youth. I want to thank Margaret Steketee. You helped me through one of the darkest moments of my adult life. Thank you. I love you for it. Special thanks to Cynthia and Brian Totten. You guys put on the best Bed and Breakfast ever and I can honestly say that my thoughts were easier to put on paper when I was at your place. Thank you. Thanks to my little league coaches and mentors, the Great Rueben Smartt, Maurice Barnes, Jimmy Carter, Robert Foster,

Johnny Walker and James Burress. Playgrounds were safe because of you and legends were cultivated under your direction. Thanks to Pastor Joe Jones of the Grand Rapids Urban League. You forced me to look at things through a different set of circumstances while challenging my intellect. I needed that. Even the mentor needs a mentor.

Thanks to Strong Fathers and Tony Jolliffi. Your Strong Fathers Program is one of the most important programs of our communities and I'm glad to be a part of it. My story may have had a different outcome if your services were available to me as a scared nineteen-year-old. I want to thank the following Southeast Grand Rapids Michigan Men for being inspiring to me as well as authors for all: Kris Mathis, Chris Sain Jr., and Eric Large. Your words helped me in more ways than you think. I was honored to turn the pages in your books and learn from my brothers.

Last but not least I have to thank three women. First...Janine Parker, our daughter is beautiful. I didn't treat you fairly when we were kids. For years, I judged you for not being a good mom. I'm sorry. I know deep down that you are a good person. To my ex-wife Stephanie. I learned a lot from you, especially about adoption. With you being an adoptee, I witnessed you reunite your two biological families successfully, and now three different families are all family because of you. Despite our break up, you have continued to be there for my children. Thank you. Last but not least I want to thank the mother of my children Mandy. I am fully aware that our relationship will always be strained. During the process of writing this book, there was a shift that took place in my thinking. For years, I referred to you as my Ex. It has such a negative connotation to it. You are so much more to me than just my Ex. You are the mother to my two children. One that you gave birth to and the other you are a mother to as if she is your own. You are doing a fantastic job of raising our son. Despite all of the bitterness that I have toward you, I do want to thank you for the morals, values and character that you have instilled in our son. Because you are the mother of my children, you are one of the most important people in my life and I will respect you as such.

This has to be said; Dads catch a bad rap for just being good dads. Our society is so far gone that we applaud dads for being average or simply doing the right thing. A single mom is expected to do so much, but a dad is viewed as a superhero for buying diapers. When did this happen? When did it become socially acceptable for a father to not be present? I don't have all of the answers but I'd be happy to be a part of the dialogue.

Currently, I run a truancy program as a Youth Development Specialist. Out of the 14 kids that are in my class, only two of them will go home to a father. As a coach, I look up in the stands and see single women cheering their sons and daughters on much more than I see fathers or couples for that matter. The kids that I coach, know that they can count on me for anything. Because of my position, I am mentoring close to 20 young boys in my program and that is not to include #TheProgram. If you are a man that has read this book then I am encouraging you to mentor at least one youth. The fatherlessness epidemic will not be solved in a year or two. In the meantime, I hope that I have at least inspired someone to be a foster parent. It is my "Thought of a Foster Dad" that foster parents hold one of the most important jobs in the world.

Bibliography

U.S. Department of Health and Human Services, Administration for Children and Families, Administration on Children, Youth and Families, Children's Bureau. The AFCARS Report. *Administration for Children and Families.* July 2015. Web. 28 December 2016.

U.S. Department of Health and Human Services, Administration for Children and Families, Administration on Children, Youth and Families, Children's Bureau. The AFCARS Report: Preliminary FY 2009 Estimates as of July 2010. *Administration for Children and Families.* July 2010. Web. 28 December 2016

U.S. Department of Health and Human Services. Child Welfare Information Gateway. Web. 28 December 2016.

Sutton, Amy. "Do Team Sports Help Kids be Successful Later in Life?" *livestrong.com.* Leaf Group, Ltd. 18 June 2015 Web. 28 December 2016.

Phelps, PhD, LCSW, Don. "Therapeutic Use of Expressive Arts with Children." *Socialworktoday.com.* Great Valley Publishing Company. Web. 28 December 2016.

Haviland, Matt and Walker, Dawn. *"The Daddy Gap."* November 7, 2014

Sain, Chris. *"Dumb Athlete."* March 20, 2014

Mathis, Kris. *"From Success to Significance: The 8 Keys to Achieving any Goal or Dream."* 2012

Julian is a Youth Development Specialist for an International Christian agency for social services with children and families. Answering God's calling, Julian works with foster care youth between the ages of thirteen and eighteen teaching employ-ability skills and leadership development for a Summer Youth Employment Program. As a foster care advocate, public speaker, and author, Julian has committed his life to encouraging loving people to become foster parents. Julian and his wife adopted two teenage boys at the age of thirteen and fifteen out of foster care. To date, Julian has been a foster dad for more than ten children.